MENTAL TOUGHNESS & MINDSET

LIFE LESSONS FROM STOICISM & ANCIENT SPARTAN PHILOSOPHY + A GUIDE ON HOW TO STOP OVERTHINKING, ESCAPE NEGATIVE THOUGHTS, RELIEVE STRESS & ANXIETY

D1509809

THOMAS SWAIN

Start Your Week The Right Way

We've all had that sinking feeling on a Sunday night, when you remember it's Monday tomorrow and the weekend is over. It can be tricky trying to launch ourselves back into work-mode, but with the right motivation and mentality, you can get your week off to the perfect start.

Receive evidence-based guidance, up-to-date resources, and first-hand accounts to help you.

Sign Up Now & You will receive this newsletter every Monday.

https://www.subscribepage.com/tswain

Scan the QR code to join.

CONTENTS

WAY OF STOIC: LIFE LESSONS FROM STOICISM TO STRENGTHEN YOUR CHARACTER, BUILD MENTAL TOUGHNESS, EMOTIONAL RESILIENCE, MINDSET, SELF-DISCIPLINE & WISDOM

OVERTHINKING: HOW TO STOP OVERTHINKING, ESCAPE NEGATIVE THOUGHTS, DECLUTTER YOUR MIND, RELIEVE STRESS & ANXIETY, BUILD MENTAL TOUGHNESS & LIVE FULLY

WAY OF THE STOIC

LIFE LESSONS FROM STOICISM TO STRENGTHEN YOUR CHARACTER, BUILD MENTAL TOUGHNESS, EMOTIONAL RESILIENCE, MINDSET, SELF DISCIPLINE & WISDOM

THOMAS SWAIN

INTRODUCTION

In the pursuit of living a better life how many self-help books have you read? How many inspirational/motivational YouTube videos have you watched? Countless I imagine. Just like me you've probably read or watched all too many. You see it's all too easy to get caught in the trap of thinking that more knowledge is the answer. But in seeking answers we often become lost in the endless stream of self-help books, gurus, videos, and motivational quotes that pop up every day. Yet rarely do they stick. In fact, many are recyclable and easily forgotten. New self-help fads come and go whilst the underlying issues persist.

For many of us, we feel like our life isn't anything special because it doesn't match the ideal standards portrayed in the media. Illusions persist of the ideal life being a series of highs. That life is about how much money you have in the bank. That life is about how to flash your lifestyle or about how much you own. Or how hot you are, or the social circles you move in. Additionally, we are now judged by how many friends we have on social media or by how many people view our stories, the number of comments or likes we receive, and so on. People are always chasing these highs. Yet we see countless celebrities with large followings and a seemingly perfect life who seek mental help or even worse cases have committed suicide. Is all that money, fame, and glamor the source of happiness?

According to Stoicism the beliefs we hold and the actions we take come from our descriptions of the world around us. All too often we value things that aren't bringing us true happiness. Now, this is all part of being human and we are still the same biological humans we were two thousand years ago when Stoicism first originated. We still face the same problems, emotions, and adversities. Therefore, Stoicism has lasted for thousands of years. It is a timeless philosophy that was originally developed to guide people to live their best lives. The basis of which is to live in alignment with nature. Essentially this means to act for the greater good of humanity because according to Stoicism all humans are connected through the universe. That God is in all of us.

Now more than ever society has become fragmented and disconnected. So many people live in isolation, spending their days working in front of a screen and their evenings alone. Too often we think we are separate from the world. Yet we are very much a part of it. However, the more we isolate the less happy we become because we are separated from the interconnectedness of our universe. When one considers themselves in isolation from our universe is when one does harm. When one realizes they are part of the universe they are living in alignment with nature. Goodness comes from understanding our place in the universe and collaborating with it for mutual benefit. This is the foundation of Stoicism which is living virtuously. Happiness is a by-product of this way of living.

Stoicism is often misunderstood as being uncaring or avoiding any pleasures. Or that it requires you to be unemotional with repressed feelings. Perhaps this misunderstanding has stopped you and many others from learning more about it. However, this is a false judgment that comes from Stoic ideas that teach us to not get carried away with irrational desires, pleasures, and fears. Stoics are not stone-cold people without feelings. Incidentally in a study of more than five hundred Stoic students observed by the Modern Stoicism organization satisfaction with life and positive emotions both increased significantly through their practices.

Indeed, feelings and emotions are all a normal part of the human experience. It's not about pretending they don't exist. We can still feel them, cry or be happy and experience those emotions. But Stoicism teaches us to not let them cloud our rational choices of what's best for our true nature. Much of the emotions and feelings that arise in us are automatic. We can do nothing about them. But we can accept them, and we do not need to act because of them. That's the difference between humans and animals. Animals act on their feelings whilst humans have the power of rational thinking. Stoicism says we should become conscious of our emotions. In doing so we can choose to not act emotionally but instead with reason. Consequently, we can choose the best way to respond to our emotions. When faced with fear or anxiety we will have the courage to act on what is best. When faced with temptation we will have the strength to do what is right.

Stoicism is a simple and easy-to-understand philosophy. Yet it is so profound. You won't need to learn a bunch of philosophy or meditate for hours on end to understand it. Neither is it a religion. What we learn from it we are not called to follow. It is up to us how we apply it to our lives and how much of it we utilize. The Stoics believed there is a divine force within the cosmos that exists beyond the reach of our human senses. They called this the Logos which is the divine reason implicit in the universe and "moves through all creation". Refusing the Logos is the root of suffering. Although their vision of God is not as a physical entity. It is instead perceived as a system of order and logic. As such Stoicism can be adapted to align with other religions whatever your beliefs may be.

Living the way of Stoicism will require a revolution in your ways of thinking and attitudes. The Stoic philosopher must abandon their ego and existing view of reality to instead see life from a more universal view. One must dig deep into the soul to redirect their external life and in turn, become happier. Often this requires a reversal of one's thinking. Our values get reassessed to be not on externals but to be from the perspective of nature. False beliefs in finding happiness in materialism or status will need to be redirected. Because when we prioritize the external ahead of virtue, we are separating our nature from the universe which connects us all. When this happens, toxic emotions come up and we become more isolated. Instead, we need to realize that happiness comes from virtuous living. Good or evil is not contained in what we desire or avoid but rather it is in our thinking and beliefs. Any decisions and actions we take are based on those beliefs.

The principles of Stoicism are powerful and useful. That's why they have stood the test of time and are still applicable to this day. For me, they have helped give purpose, meaning, and direction to my life. I am Thomas Swain, a bestselling author, and brand manager of History Brought Alive. I promise you that through Stoicism you can attain inner peace, overcome adversity, become aware of your impulses, and learn how to respond correctly. You will learn to appreciate what you have, to find true joy and happiness in life. One can learn to manage negative situations of loss, depressing thoughts, and even face your fears. You will see that happiness can come from the smallest things. When we break free from our attachments. When we let go of outcomes. When we learn how to control our emotions and take the right pathway, we can enjoy the deepest ocean of happiness.

Maybe you're lost right now, and you are seeking more meaning. Or maybe you're going through a rough time. Stoicism can help you. Whether you are a student, executive, or just a curious person it will teach you to live your best life. Questions of how to live your best life will be answered. Questions of how to deal with what life throws at you will be dealt with. Along with dealing with desires and much, much more. You will learn to make better decisions based on logic and experience. This can help you in your career, studies, and personal life. Ultimately it will guide you to a better life. The result is wisdom, inner tranquility, and peace. In turn, you will be more at ease with yourself whatever your past experiences are.

The future is better with Stoicism because you can improve your overall life experience. Negative emotions can be effectively dealt with using its ancient and proven strategies from the greatest legends of history. A strong mindset is a key, and you will find how in this book. Not only can it help us in rough patches or crises, but it can also help us to cultivate a strong character with a clear head to deal with life and any rough patches or crises. In the modern world it will help to improve your state of mind and in turn your overall life. Without a life philosophy to guide us we succumb to the whims of others and to the turmoil of life. Stoicism is the best life philosophy out there. Again, it is one that has stood the test of time for thousands of years.

THE GOLDEN AGE

Zeno of Citium was the first person to introduce Stoicism to Athens circa 300 BC. A student of Plato's Academy, he was influenced by early Greek philosophy which he later developed into early Stoic philosophy. Some years later his ideas were further developed by philosophers in ancient Greece and then by the Roman Stoics. Famous philosophers, Seneca, Epictetus, and the Roman Emperor Marcus Aurelius can be credited with developing Stoicism. This was the golden age of Stoicism and it lasted for about one hundred years. In later centuries changes in culture and politics shifted away from philosophical thinking. Stoicism remained largely forgotten about until a modern-day revival.

In the beginning Stoicism was a system of complicated ideas involving logic, physics, grammar, meteorology and so on. Early Stoic philosophers focused on cosmic order and nature.

The Roman Stoics later developed these ideas into ways of better living. Back then, society was evolving and people wanted to live a better life. One didn't assume that attaining prestige, wealth or beauty would necessarily bring them happiness. People wanted something more meaningful and coming from a deeper place. Increasing life satisfaction through ways of thinking and behavior was a keyway to improve their life appreciation. Stoicism provided the answers to stress, fear, anxiety, and the trials of the human condition.

Who Were the Ancient Stoics?

Even though it started many years ago Stoicism has lasted until this day which is testament to its value. Throughout history there have been numerous famous Stoic philosophers but here we will explore the most important ones from ancient times.

Zeno of Citium

Zeno of Citium is attributed with starting Stoicism. By all accounts he was a wealthy trader. During one of his sea voyages, his ship was wrecked, and he lost all of the cargo. Later in life he realized that his perceived bad fortune of being shipwrecked had actually become something much more fortunate. With no boat or money, he ended up in Athens where he discovered the philosophy of Socrates and Plato. Inspired by their teachings he developed their philosophies into early Stoicism.

Zeno began teaching Stoicism at the Ancient Agora of Athens where he founded one of the leading philosophical schools of the time. Much of what we know about him is from the book, Lives and Opinions of Eminent Philosophers by Diogenes Laertius. Indeed, Stoicism has developed a lot since he began to outline the philosophy, but the fundamentals have stayed the same. As he would say "happiness is a good flow of life." That is achieved through the peace of mind which is the result of living a life of virtue in accordance with reason and nature.

Marcus Aurelius

Marcus Aurelius The Roman Emperor is probably one of the most famous Stoics from history. Born almost two thousand years ago into a prestigious family he would later become emperor of Rome which he led for almost two decades. During his reign he experienced wars with the Parthian Empire and many other attacks on the Empire. Furthermore, he was in the midst of the rise of Christianity, a plague that left many dead and much more turmoil during his reign.

Marcus left behind a personal diary which we know all know as his Meditations. Inside are the private thoughts of the most powerful man in the world at that time. Meditations reveals his own personal philosophy and brand of Stoicism. In his writing he explores how to be more virtuous, just, wiser and immune to temptation. It is a defining book on building character, self-discipline, ethics, self-actualization, humility, and strength. Naturally being a Roman Emperor during that time would have been a great position of prestige to be in. If he wished to, he could do or have almost anything. Essentially any desire could be satisfied, and nothing was off limits to an emperor. Yet he proved to be a noble and worthy man of his position.

"Waste no more time arguing what a good man should be.
Be one." - Marcus Aurelius

Seneca

Seneca was born in the south of Spain over two thousand years ago. Educated in Rome he was the son of Seneca the Elder, a prestigious Roman writer. Seneca started out his career in politics and rose to become a top financial clerk. Later in life he experienced a changing of fortunes when

Claudius, the new emperor of Rome accused of adultery with his niece. Seneca was exiled to the island of Corsica. After eight years of exile, Agrippina, the wife of Claudius, negotiated permission for him to return and tutor her son Nero. Nero would later become one of the most infamous and tyrannical emperors in the history of Rome. Seneca was by his side as an advisor to help run the government and affairs of the state. However, as Nero became more paranoid their relationship declined and Seneca's eventual death came by the orders of Nero himself.

Throughout all those turbulent times in Seneca's life Stoicism was the constant. His collection of letters is one of the most well-known works from Stoic philosophy. Inside can be found ways to conduct oneself, relationships, live a good life, approach adversity or death, and develop awareness of one's emotions. This is accessible for men and women from all backgrounds.

"We are not given a short life, but we make it short, and we are not ill-supplied but wasteful of it." - Seneca.

Epictetus

Born a slave to a wealthy household Epictetus would later rise to become a famous Stoic philosopher. Mistreatment during his time as a slave had left him crippled and walking with a limp. His suffering motivated him to develop the concepts of Stoicism. Later on in life he was granted his freedom and began teaching philosophy in Rome where he continued to teach for over twenty years. During this time, he was a major influence on Marcus Aurelius along with many other powerful men and women. Eventually his teaching in Rome ended when the emperor Domitian famously banned all philosophers there. Consequently, Epictetus relocated to Nicopolis in Greece where he established a school of philosophy which he taught at until his last days.

Many people throughout history and to this day find comfort in the ancient lessons of Epictetus. They draw strength from knowing that whatever is done to them is outside their control but at the same time they always have control over their mind. No one can take this away. Epictetus's Stoic philosophy was not only theoretical but also had real practical application to people from all backgrounds and walks of life. Yet he never actually wrote anything down. Arrian, his student, is to thank for the written accounts we have of his lessons.

"To make the best of what is in our power and take the rest as it occurs." - Epictetus

FOUNDATIONS

At the center of Stoicism is a universe which guides and connects us all to each other. The universe is vast and infinite. From the landscape to the earth, to the stars and the sky. It is all encompassing and includes all living things. We are all connected through it. Any imperfection comes from a misunderstanding of its parts which includes the humans who inhabit it. When one considers themselves in isolation from our universe is when one does harm. When one realizes they are part of the universe they are living in alignment with nature. Goodness comes from understanding our place in the universe and collaborating with it for mutual benefit. This is the foundation of Stoicism.

Nature in Stoicism is the measure of all things. It gives us guidance as a pathway to excellence. Through nature we develop reason and that transforms our understanding of ourselves. Zeno taught his students that we all have an inner genius and purpose which connects us to the universe. God is in all things and shares his divinity through all of it. The premise of living in alignment with nature concerns behaving as a rational human being rather than behaving out of passion as a wild beast would. Rational is what separates us from other animals. Applying our ability to reason towards our actions ensures that we live in alignment with nature.

Oikeiôsis

The Stoics developed the theory of "Oikeiôsis", to explain how reason transforms the world view of humans. According to this theory humans have two stages of development. The first is our initial impulse of self-love. In fact, all living organisms share this impulse. Whilst some are indeed more primitive the theory states that the first impulse is the awareness of a living organism recognizing that its body belongs to itself. As a result, it is compelled to preserve itself by pursuing things that improve its wellbeing whilst avoiding those that don't. For example, a plant grows towards sunlight. A baby craves milk and so on. Literally, it concerns the process of making something one's own. Everything in nature has its own set of responsibilities and unique character. For example, an animal must care for its offspring otherwise it neglects its duties of living in alignment with nature. This is actualized in its displays of making self-preservation its main goal. Whilst for human beings living in alignment with nature is something much more complex because we have the capacity for reason.

As humans grow, they continue to love themself and then through adolescence their ability for reason begins to evolve. From birth children are biologically wired to preserve themselves. Their motivation is towards pleasure and away from pain. As we age, we expand our consciousness to being a son or daughter, sister or brother, friend, citizen and so on. Essentially our biology extends to wanting to preserve this expansion because we now have a duty or obligation to them. Parents, siblings and friends are treated with care as an extension of oneself. Oikeiosis expands out into the human race albeit in an increasingly diluted measure. Our natural Oikeiosis towards others is the foundation of how well we integrate into the universe. It is our affinity with the entire human race and the universe itself. The final stage which is the goal of Stoicism is to live in alignment with nature.

The Happiness Triangle

Living in alignment with nature for Stoics is the most well-known definition of living the good life. But what exactly does it mean? Ultimately the goal of life according to Stoicism is

Eudaimonia. In Greek this means to flourish. Essentially it is the full attainment of happiness or living the good life. The happiness triangle is a simple and visual way of explaining this concept.

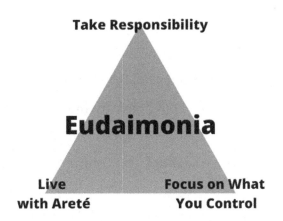

Eudaimonia

At the center of the triangle is Eudaimonia which is the ultimate goal of life. In simple terms it is to have supreme happiness or to thrive. Achieving this comes through living in alignment with the other three parts of the Stoic Happiness Triangle. Which can be interpreted as living in alignment with nature.

Live with Areté

To live with Areté is to become the best version of yourself right now. According to Stoicism character and actions are more important than status or materialism. Stoicism welcomes everybody regardless of their background, circumstance or appearance. The real beauty of life comes from excellence of mind and character. Not the physical. Character is our only real possession. Everything else can be taken away.

Cultivating your character is the highest good. The ideal character is someone who lives in harmony with himself, other humans and nature. They have serenity and follow reason. Whatever fate comes to them they accept graciously and realize it is beyond their control. They rise above desire and emotion to achieve peace of mind. Death is not something they fear. They are honorable and have strong self-discipline, wisdom, justice and courage and self-discipline. Continually asking questions of yourself can help you to live this way. For example:

- What is the right thing to do here?
- What would the perfect friend, father or brother do?
- How can I be my best at this moment?
- If I were developed to my maximum potential and living my best life, how would it look? Am I living up to that?
- What is the gap between who I am now and my best self?
- How can I close that gap?

We must make the time to work on improving ourselves and becoming better. As you become better you will lift up those around you and ultimately make the world a better place. That's not about being selfish. Afterall improving yourself is about transcending desire and serving others. Now that isn't selfish. Life is larger than the individual. In order to become our happiest and to thrive in life we need to express the best version of ourselves in each and every moment. Align with your deep values and act accordingly.

Stoicism focuses on not pointing out the faults of others but rather of improving our own faults for the benefit of others. As a result, we learn how to think better, to better prepare for challenges, to live more virtuously and to remove toxicity. We must be on a pathway of continuous improvement. There is always a deeper work going on within ourselves. Throughout the challenges and setbacks of life we should always be improving. Progress in life brings stability to us and as a by-product it benefits those around us.

"A good character is the only guarantee of everlasting, carefree happiness." – Seneca

A good role model will help you to measure your character. Find people whose way of life matches their words and character. This is the kind of person who would be a great role model. Now you don't necessarily need to know them in person. It could be someone you know through books, videos and so on. It could even be an ancient Stoic like the great Seneca or the emperor Marcus Aurelius. Whoever it is they should be a person of high virtue and moral standing. Let them be your guardian. How would they react to such situations? How would they behave in your situation? It is important to note here that you don't compare yourself to them. We are all different. Simply let them guide you. Allow their influence to guide your decisions and for them to be your guardian.

"If a companion is dirty, his friends cannot help but get a little dirty too, no matter how clean they started out." -
Epictetus

Focus on what you control

Focus on what you control, this is a prominent principle of Stoicism. Living a good life requires focusing on what we control and accepting the rest as it happens. We can't change some things, but we can change how we respond. Other people's opinions, our reputations, possessions and even our own body we cannot control. In order to live a good life, we must focus on the things we can control. When we try to control those things we cannot, it leads to anxiety, stress and worry. Indeed, there are many things we cannot control. But there are many we do. Living with Areté is something we can control. The past or future we don't control. However, in the present moment we can focus and make our best life. William Irvine identified three levels of influence we have.

- High influence - the choices, judgments and actions we take
- Partial influence - our relationships, health, wealth and behaviors
- No influence - external circumstances

"Of things some are in our power, and others are not." - *Epictetus*

Take responsibility

You are responsible for yourself and that includes your own happiness. Take responsibility for living your best life and achieving Eudaimonia. Take responsibility instead of blaming others or your circumstances. This will free you from being mentally enslaved to the opinions of others. No more being a victim. Because when we take responsibility for ourselves, we become more powerful. We choose how to react and decide on what things mean to us. As a result, we become less upset about what happens or what doesn't happen. You are the only one who has access to your own mind. No one else. Take responsibility for who you are and how you live one hundred percent. Taking responsibility for your life puts you at the cause and not the effect. Doing this changes your energy and puts you onto a higher vibration. It is that energy that affects our thoughts, actions and feelings. The higher those are the better.

When you find yourself in the face of a challenge do you blame others, or do you take responsibility? Accept the situation as it is. Observe and see what is in your control and what is not. Accept what is not and then make the most of improving what you control. That is your responsibility. When you blame others, you hand over that responsibility along with your emotions to them. No improvement of oneself is possible from there. One becomes a victim of life. So, wouldn't it be better to be in control of your life? Indeed, this is possible when you take responsibility for it.

"If you want anything good, you must get it from yourself" - *Epictetus*

THE PATHWAY TO HAPPINESS

The Ancient Stoics believed that the pathway to true happiness could be found through virtue. A virtuous life is about excelling in our human nature. To be free of passions that disturb the soul and to have rational understanding of one's responsibilities. Pursuing a path of virtue involves taming our desires, impulses and aversions. Happiness and living a good life are byproducts of living virtuously. Virtue in Stoicism is distinguished as anything which contributes to happiness. Whilst vice is anything which contributes to misery. Vice is ignorance whilst virtue is knowledge. Vice is dominated by strong and irrational emotions otherwise known as passions. Between virtue and vice is a gray area known as the indifferents. Now these aren't necessarily good nor bad, they are just preferred or dispreferred. The problem is that many of us misjudge indifferents and act contrary to nature. For example, when it comes to wealth. A person with bad judgment would be likely to act greedily and desire to be richer than is enough. In the process of attaining more riches they might neglect others and as such they act selfishly. Furthermore, if they lost their wealth then they would probably end up being more miserable.

Most of us associate happiness with the concept of having more. Whether that's more money, beauty, fame and so on we are led to believe it will make us happier. But Stoicism teaches us that less is in fact more. When we want more, we become a slave to our desires. When we want less, we can free ourselves from our desires. Sure, it's good to have possessions and to want more. A better house, a better car, more money and so on. We can appreciate the pursuit and acclaim of those. We care for them, but we do not fear their loss because ultimately, they are indifferent. Happiness does not come from having more things. Even if we get all that we want it will still never be enough. Now don't mistake this conceptualization as being a person without feelings. No that is not the case. Instead, it is the ability to distinguish what brings true happiness and what does not. That is to understand the difference between virtue and vice.

- Virtue: Wisdom, Justice, Courage, Moderation.

- Vice: Foolishness, Injustice, Cowardice, Intemperance.
- Indifferents: Reputation, Beauty, Health, Wealth.

Wisdom

At the root of virtue is wisdom. It is the way of knowing what needs to be done and what must not be done. It is the knowledge of what is bad or good, or the knowledge of what brings true happiness. Such knowledge helps us to understand the world around us in a much more accurate way. Then we can make better judgments and decisions based on our experiences and knowledge. Those decisions shape how well we live according to nature.

Stoicism holds the belief that a wise man can be his own counsel and that anybody can make progress towards wisdom. Through wisdom we can discover more virtuous qualities including soundness of judgment, shrewdness, sensibleness and circumspection. The opposite of wisdom is ignorance.

"Without wisdom the mind is sick, and the body itself, however physically powerful, can only have the kind of strength that is found in a person in a demented or delirious

state." - Seneca

Justice

Marcus Aurelius held justice as being the most important value. For him it was the source of the other values. Justice also known as morality is about doing what is the right and fair thing to do. Even in times of adversity or weakness. Our sense of justice dictates how we act towards others and how well we live in alignment with nature. Justice creates more fairness for everyone. It can be thought of as one's moral compass which helps us to focus not just on actions better for oneself but on actions that are better for us all.

Stoicism teaches us that we are all one and that no one should harm another. That we are not born just to serve ourselves but for the common good of mankind. So that when we act for the common good it is justice being served. Are we acting respectfully, with kindness and fair treatment? Do we give or do we just take? When we damage the community, ultimately, we hurt ourselves. On the opposite side of justice would be doing wrong to another person, living in chaos and acting selfishly.

"What is not good for the beehive, cannot be good for the bees." - Marcus Aurelius

Courage

Courage stands at the opposite side of cowardice. It's about doing the right thing even when we are afraid to do it. One does their duty despite any fear. Having courage helps us to overcome our weaknesses and to live virtuously. Those with courage still feel fear, anxiety and desire but it is courage that helps them to act in the right way despite those fears. Often our initial reaction when confronted with fear is to panic. Fear can take over our rational mind. But the courageous ones do not hold onto these initial reactions. Instead, they go beyond them.

Without persistence we are unable to endure any hardships on our way to a goal and as such we may give into sinful vices. Courage is not just about facing our fears it is also about having indifference to external situations. Ultimately courage will guide us to being able to do what's right in spite of any reservations and fears. Actualized courage can be seen as Marcus Aurelius struggling to overcome the corruptions of absolute power. To be a good man even whilst Rome was at the height of decadence and decline. It's about the fighter going out to battle in the face of fear. Each conquest requires courage and the process in turn builds more courage. Take action, take risks and gain the rewards.

"Two words should be committed to memory and obeyed, "persist and resist." - Epictetus

Moderation

Moderation is about knowing that real abundance comes from having only what is essential. When faced with temptation it helps us to defend against fleeting pleasures, pains and false realities. One is cautious about what they should and should not do in the face of desire. It is a way of knowing whether or not things are worthy of choosing or of avoiding. In modern times one might associate this with being mindful or of having moral consciousness.

Viewing matters in a detached way helps us to be more objective and to in turn do the right thing. In reality it can be actualized as controlling oneself from overindulging whether that be in eating, vices, thinking and so on. In turn we can benefit from long-term satisfaction over short-term fleeting pleasures. We can be free from materialism, extreme behavior, impulses, cravings and addictions. This helps us to thrive and live in abundance when we practice it correctly. Ultimately, it's about doing whatever is essential and necessary. Nothing more.

Stoicism teaches us to practice moderation in everything from wealth, appetite, indulgence and life. Especially these days in dopamine driven social media and life on demand we can benefit from it more than ever. We can stop ourselves from falling into the hands of greed, laziness and addictive behaviors. Through moderation we can attain more positive benefits including modesty, orderliness and self-mastery. The opposite of moderation is greed, addiction, instant gratification, laziness, and procrastination.

"Most of what we say and do is unnecessary. So, in every case one should prompt oneself: 'Is this, or is it not, something necessary?' - Marcus Aurelius

Living Virtuously

Early Stoics were taught to think clearly, make decisions with speed and to have no regret after deciding. Epictetus advised his students when making decisions to be mindful of what is in their control. First understand what it is you face. Is it under your control or not? Once you have determined what is in your control you can start to think clearly about it. Next determine if it is of virtue. Pass it through the four cardinal virtues. If it is something of virtue, then do it. Whilst if it is not, then don't do it. Really decisions can be that simple!

For anything indifferent, consider if they are preferred indifferents. This includes things such as good health, wealth, beauty, strength, reputation and so on. Whilst those dispreferred indifferents which are contrary to nature include things such as death, weakness, pain, disease, poverty and so on. In most cases it is better to avoid them but, in some cases, we have to stay virtuous and deal with them appropriately which would be to behave with indifference towards them. Realize that they are often temporary and do not affect our control of our inner being. The virtuous use of indifferents will lead to a happy life. Whilst using them wrongly will make one unhappy.

Take effective action. Only take action once you have assessed a situation. Take the time to think, plan and reflect before you dive into something. Consider the consequences, the pros and the cons. good decisions depend on the time spent considering the right course of action. Obviously, you don't want to get bogged down in too much thinking but just make sure you have at least put in some thought before you act. Look before you leap so to say. For big decisions it's a good idea to have it all written down so your mind doesn't go in circles and can work more creatively.

When a person becomes an adult with reason, they have the ability to perform "appropriate acts." Stoicism defines an appropriate act as being "that which reason persuades one to do" or "that which when done admits of reasonable justification." Each action we take must be authentic to our moral integrity. That requires one to understand the actions he takes and the impact of them not being just on his life but within the universe. Most people act selfishly and do not conform to the laws of life as a whole with respect to all of the virtues. To help understand our actions we can lay them out on a scale from vicious to virtuous.

1. Actions against the appropriate act
    A. For example, neglecting one's family, not treating others with kindness, squandering wealth or health in the wrong circumstances.
2. Intermediate appropriate actions which although are proper conduct but are not consistent with all four virtues

A. For example, people pleasing, doing something for the benefit of one collective but at the same time it negatively impacts others.

3. Perfect acts performed consistently with rational

A. This is virtuous.

We are not born sinful or corrupt, but we are born with resources to thrive in life. All of us have the seeds of virtue within us and it is our responsibility to bring them out. Yes, we all have different starting points. Throughout life we will be presented with obstacles, distractions and bad situations but we have the choice on how we respond to them. Our inborn tools and efforts determine ultimately where we will go. Living according to these virtues is the goal of Stoicism and it is progress towards living in alignment with nature.

Choose to thrive and live happily by living virtuously. Virtue in itself is its own reward. It is not about doing something because it feels good. Rather it's about acting in alignment with nature to be virtuous. Putting the knowledge of these four virtues into practice is paramount. It will help you to know how to respond in various situations. Whatever that situation is. Whether it be a positive or negative situation, one can choose to respond with virtue. Ask yourself questions before taking any action and let the virtues of Stoicism reveal the answers for you. Through practicing virtue, you can achieve happiness, success, honor, praise, love and live in alignment with nature. In the end it is your happiness and quality of life that depend on it.

THE DICHOTOMY OF CONTROL & ACCEPTING YOUR FATE

The Dichotomy of Control is one of the most popular teachings of Stoicism. All things in life can be divided into what we control and what we do not control. Wisdom is knowing what we control and what we do not control. Realize that what we control is very limited. It would be foolish and narcissistic to assume everything is within your control. Trying to control things which you cannot, will also drive you insane. Emotional suffering is the result of people placing too much importance on things beyond their control. Stress is unnecessarily caused because simply it is not possible to change those things. Attachment to them makes us a slave to them. When things don't go your way emotions can spiral out of control since they are attached to something you don't control. Ultimately the most important thing within your control is your inner world.

Modern psychology recognizes the value of understanding the boundaries between what we can and cannot control. Happiness is around forty percent dependent on what we can control. Whilst just ten to twenty percent comes from external circumstances. The remaining forty percent of one's happiness requirement is within us. Knowing this it's possible to work on significantly improving one's overall happiness even if you are naturally pessimistic.

Regardless of external circumstances anyone can indeed be happier. First of all, realize that there are things you can control and those that you cannot. Essentially our inner world is what we can control. The majority of things in this world are out of your control. You have no control over what kind of family you're born into. You cannot control the economy, diseases, the weather and so on. Ultimately, we don't control what happens to us or even to our own bodies. People will have their opinions and you cannot control those either. Everyone has their own unique opinion. Whilst some might think your amazing others will think much less of you. There isn't much you can do to change that opinion. However, you can choose to not let it affect you because your own internal reaction is within your control.

We cannot control this crazy world, but we can control how we respond to it. Remind yourself of this every day. Let go of emotional attachment to wanting things to happen a certain way. Waste no more time complaining about things you do not control or trying to control them. Peace comes from accepting this and letting go of what we cannot control. Unhappiness comes from trying to control what we can't. Understanding this will help you to move through the world with ease. Changing ourselves is easier than trying to change the world. Be the change you want to see in the world. Understanding this will bring you strength and wisdom. When you try to control those things often it brings unhappiness. Instead focus on what you have control over which are your thoughts, judgements and actions.

The archer analogy in Stoic philosophy explains this well. The goal of the archer is to hit the target. Some things he has control over. For example, he has control over his choice of bow and arrow, his training, his aim and when to shoot. He can do his best with all of these elements. But whether or not he hits the target is ultimately out of his power. At any moment the wind could come and cause him to miss. He has to be willing to accept all of the possible outcomes. In doing so he has to accept that he has done his very best. The rest is upto the universe. Believe and always do your very best. Leave the rest to nature. If it is meant to be then it will be. All we can do is our best, let go of attachment to the result and to accept whatever happens.

"You have power over your mind-not outside events. Realize this and you will find strength." –Marcus Aurelius

Amor Fati (love of fate)

Stoicism calls upon us to be responsible for ourselves and to learn to accept the way things are. For example, getting angry in traffic for taking too long will not help to speed things up. It already happened and you cannot control it. Accept it. Our perception of what happens to us is in our control. We can decide if something is good, bad or indifferent. Learn how to differentiate between them. Then focus on appropriate reactions and actions from you. That is where your true power is. When you understand what you can and control it allows you to focus energy on what matters which are your thoughts and actions.

The ancient Stoics were big believers in fate and the powers of divination. They called this Amor Fati which essentially means, the love of fate. We have to accept that what happens is beyond our control. When we learn to accept what happens we go beyond accepting whatever happens to loving whatever happens. Realize that something greater than you is controlling your fate. Realize that it might be a step towards something much more favorable for you. Love that. This is Amor Fati.

According to Stoicism everything that happens is already predetermined and Stoic ethics dictate that human happiness is caused by conforming with the predetermined plan. Otherwise known as living in alignment with nature/God's plan. However, they also argue that we all have countless different realities which depend on the choices we make and the paths we choose to follow. Our destinies are written but we have free will. If we live in alignment with nature, then we will realize our destiny which is to live our best life.

Now some might say that if our outcomes are already fixed then why bother? If it is already fated, what is the point? The Stoic would answer that sequences and events are co-fated. The big events in our lives such as the day we die and the day we are born are fated. It is our individual character which causes us to decline or to take the best actions presented to us. Socrates knew through a dream that he would die within captivity in three days' time. He chose to accept God's plan and to not resist it. If he were to act against nature maybe, he would have escaped. But regardless he would still have died in three days' time. Choosing morality will align you with determinism. Within this framework we can make the right decisions and meet our best fate.

Outcomes still depend on your actions which you control. If you sit there and do nothing it won't bring you a good life. Stoicism requires you to take the right action. Remember it's not about being passive with no ambition. Thinking ahead and devising the best strategy for achieving what you want is necessary. Marcus Aurelius faced plagues and many misfortunes outside of his control, but he prevailed. Otherwise, Rome would have fallen. Imagine the metaphor the Stoics often used of a dog moving along tied to a cart. The dog can enjoy the walk with the cart even though he is not in control of it, or he can resist it and be dragged along by it. We too have the choice to accept our fate or to be dragged along by it. In both scenarios we end up at the same destination, but one has a worse experience than the other.

Stoics take action. They don't just sit there and think about living a good life. They go out there and practice it through taking the right actions. We must continue to move forwards towards our goals. We may expect a certain outcome, but we might get something much better. Focus on the process of taking action and enjoy the journey. This is within your control. When things go beyond our control, we still have the control of how to respond. Focus on doing your best. Stoicism teaches us to take action without thought for future rewards. There are three premises to taking action. One is to guard ourselves from acting out of impulse. Two is to be mindful of the actions we take. Then number three is to remain detached from the results of taking action. When it comes to the results, accept them for whatever they are. Ultimately events in the external world are beyond your control. It is therefore better to accept them as they come.

"Fate leads the willing, and drags along the reluctant," -
Seneca

As Stoics we are supposed to do what is right and to do our best. We are also supposed to accept whatever happens. Seneca defined this as "I will sail across the ocean, if nothing prevents me." This is the key to building confidence and trust. Have faith that you know you have done your best and the result is out of your control. Accept the result whatever it is and continue to act in alliance with virtue. This is the process. Along the way you can adapt and change the plan when circumstances change. Everything that happens was meant to be. Keep moving forward and you will see that what you might think is bad will become good.

Nothing is more powerful in Stoicism than the realization of the dichotomy of control. Internalize your understanding of it because it will help you greatly in life. It is simple to understand but it can be difficult to practice. When we are going through tough times it can make things more manageable to remind ourselves of what we have control over. This takes our attention away from the perceived problem and focuses it onto what we do control. Letting go of the fantasy of being in control allows us to deal with life much more effectively. Everything that happens can be endured or not. Either endure it or stop complaining. Do not waste your time on things you do not control. Accept what comes your way and realize it is helping you to grow in the long run. We come again to Amor Fati which is the loving acceptance of one's fate.

SOCIETY, RELATIONSHIPS & LOVE

Thousands of years ago in ancient Rome, Antipater's successor Panaetius underlined the importance of not doing things only for personal gain but also for the common good of human society. At the time this was a poignant message in what was a corrupt society overrun with self-interest. Whatever walk of life we are from our actions can bring benefits to others. Exercising care and concern for the universe helps us to live our best lives. Caring for the universe means we also care for ourselves because we are all one. When humans think universally for the whole community and live according to the four cardinal virtues they are living in alignment with nature.

A unified rational self was one of the main beliefs of the Stoics and maintaining that unity was paramount to them. Blaming others would be a diversion from unity and that would be a mistake. This is how conflicts arise. Most of it is failing to have empathy or to understand another's point of view without judgment or false impressions. We must be in harmony with our universal nature. A golden Stoic rule is that "no man is an island". Realize that our own individual interests are intertwined with those interests and concerns of others. If we focus only on ourselves then we will suffer and fail because we are acting selfishly and against humanity. Stay connected with others and treat them as well as kindly you would yourself. Our personal development relies on being of service to others. Treat family as your own, friends as family, strangers as friends and so on. Bringing the circle of others' lives closer to our own brings us closer to living in alignment with nature.

The basis of Stoic 'philanthropy' is our love for the fellow humans of our universe. Remember that we were all created for one another. Realize that we are all part of a larger entity. Marcus Aurelius suggested that we see ourselves as a limb of a larger body. Let this guide your thoughts, actions and life. Realizing that we are all connected is virtuous and crucial to living a good life. Stoicism advocates that we expand ourselves to encompass others. As explained earlier they call this Oikeiôsis. Our goals should incorporate the greater good of humanity because that is virtuous. Undoubtedly this will lead us to more kindness.

Stoicism teaches us to act in service of others without seeking for gain, praise or recognition. Since we are all connected through the universe it is in our nature to act in such an altruistic way. Taking is insatiable to meet one's satisfaction but giving is limitless to how much satisfaction it can offer. Zeno the original Stoic philosopher underlined the importance of duty and obligation to our family and society as being of high importance. According to his teachings we should do good things for other people without desire for reward or praise. When we act for the common good of humanity it is also better for us. Do good for the sake of it and expect nothing in return. Virtue will be your reward.

Become better and lift the world up with you because the more you develop yourself the better you can serve society. Even though it can be difficult and challenging, ultimately it will bring you greater joy than selfish pursuits of passion. Now your contribution doesn't necessarily need to be a grand gesture. It can be small things that help other people's lives. Think of it like random acts of daily kindness. Or charitable projects that you're involved in. Keep thinking about ways to improve the lives of others and the community. Always be on the lookout for how to make a difference. Be the shoulder to cry on. Be the friend who listens. Be kind and be of service. Help others when you see they are in need. Perhaps you can go out to volunteer or make a donation to charity. Take every opportunity to show your kindness. Make someone's day. Make a list of all the acts of kindness you do. From big to small. It could be something as small as a smile, a compliment or even holding the door open for someone. But remember to do it without seeking reward or praise. Do not brag about it or show off. Just do it for the simple act of being kind.

Indeed, it might seem somewhat overwhelming to be responsible for others whilst you struggle with your own personal responsibility. But simply it is about having responsibility for the greater good. To not act selfishly, to think of how your emotions and actions impact others. Doing the contrary is to go against nature which is not virtuous and will ultimately bring sadness and negativity. Aimlessly chasing your own desires and pleasures is a recipe for a lonely life and one that is without virtue. Serving others and making contributions to humanity are the keys to living a good life.

But what about when other people do you wrong? The ancient Stoics were of the belief that people do not act wrongly on purpose. They believed that people act in the way that they think is best for them. However sometimes they are not truly aware of what is right for them. Therefore, we should not blame them but rather we should have empathy for them. We are all born with a blank canvas. Throughout our lives we soak up information, emotions and experiences. Our brains map everything out and we start to become shaped by our environment and life. These culminate to make all of us very different and unique in our own ways. Indeed, some of us are raised in less favorable pathways. Some of us experienced rough childhoods, bad situations, lifestyles and influences along our individual journeys. To understand each other we need to realize empathy and compassion. When we become more compassionate, we can relate with and understand each other much better. Ultimately it enhances our concept of unity with others because it helps us to understand them better. Stoics appreciate the differences of others to understand their values and beliefs. This is the power of empathy. To be able to deeply feel and understand another person.

"What brings no benefit to the hive brings none to the bee" - Marcus Aurelius

Relationships

Friendship

In Stoicism relationships based on natural feelings are healthy and should be cultivated. But those based on passion, dependency or without reason should be avoided. Friendship was valued by them, but it was also understood that friendship comes with certain tensions. Indeed, they can be fulfilling but they can also lead to dependency. True friendship is only possible after taking out attachments wherein people are not just friends to gain something. Again, it's not about cutting ties from other humans and living in solitude. Just be aware that everything is fleeting, and nothing lasts forever. Don't get attached to or hold onto people. Such behavior is possessive, and it ultimately leads to misery. Embrace and accept that life is impermanent.

Remember that the people you surround yourself with are who you become like. When you're around them for long enough you will start to talk, think and act like them. Take careful consideration of who you associate with. Choose people who want to be better humans. Who are ambitious and living the lives you aspire to? Or maybe they aren't successful now, but they have the motivation and drive to become better. Weigh carefully the people in your life. Surround yourself with great people and you too will become great because they will lift you up. Make sure they are people who you aspire to be like. Are the people you associate with lifting you up? Do they inspire you? Do you want to be like them? Yes, should be the answer here. Otherwise, it's time to meet some new people. In the end it's better to be alone than in bad company because keeping bad company is toxic.

Love & Lust

In modern society a great deal of importance has been placed on romance and love. Movies and media portray idealistic representations of romantic love. But some people live for it and the problem with that is that they are in pursuit. Love we can give freely without expecting anything in return. But love is unnatural and unnecessary. Nature doesn't make us desire love but rather it is society that does. Love is an obsession to fulfill a desire. It might seem wonderful, but it often brings pain. Once a loved one is absent, one becomes obsessed with missing them.

Lust on the other hand is a desire which is out of our control. In states of lust, we crave for another person and that makes us a slave to that desire because we cannot control that other human. Now that doesn't mean we should completely try to abandon lust. For example, sex is a form of lust, and it is seen as a preferred indifferent. Meaning that it is natural, but it is also unnecessary. We do not have to avoid it, but we should be careful not to overwhelm ourselves or do wrong things because of it. For example, to not be impulsive which often leads to regret. The levelheaded Stoic realizes that sex can disturb one's mind when mishandled which can make them act incorrectly. However, they realize that sex is something humans will do anyway. Therefore, it should be arranged to produce the least pain and most joy possible.

When couples first fall in love, they get caught up in a period of infatuation otherwise known as "the honeymoon phase". Generally, this doesn't last for long and all too often during this phase couples neglect to see each other objectively. As such they usually are blindsided by significant flaws or compatibility issues. When the honeymoon phase wears off couples are left facing these flaws and or compatibility issues. This can be avoided by taking things more slowly and getting to understand a person's nature without getting caught up in lust, craving or neediness. Avoid that desire to want or cling to another person. Keep your life filled with other things and not just that attachment to the person.

When a couple goes beyond the honeymoon phase and stays together is when a lasting relationship begins to form. This is based on companionship, trust, honesty and friendship. One should only commit to someone if they meet those criteria. Stoicism teaches us to have healthy relationships without clinging or lust. For single people Stoicism teaches us to be as pure as possible before marriage. If one does choose to indulge in pleasures, then they should do so with respect for and not to hurt others. One can have everything in moderation. Again, behave as if you were at a banquet. If something is passed to you, take a portion of it. If it has not yet come to you then wait.

Incidentally many schools of Stoicism teach that monogamy is unnatural and not beneficial to being happy. They state that men in particular should focus on more than one partner so that they can avoid the psychological obsessions and traps of love. Now please don't misunderstand this as being misogynistic. Try to look at it objectively without any illusions. Essentially, it's about not clinging to a person because as you know they are not in your control. Tranquility of the soul depends upon releasing ourselves from attachments to objects or people. Polygamy releases one from attachment and this reduces feelings of possessiveness or jealousy.

When a couple is in a monogamous relationship there must be concern and companionship for each other. Through the good and the bad times, they must stand by each other. When one person seeks to fulfill their own interest with neglect for their partner then the relationship fails. Ultimately there is no guarantee a relationship will last forever. Like everything in life, it is impermanent. Stoicism thousands of years ago taught the concept of letting go. They called it the "art of acquiescence". Essentially it is about giving up certain things and assenting so that they can be what they are to become. This is not so easy to achieve. After all we are humans and naturally, we all can get attached. Again, it's about realizing things are outside of our control. Detach from that ego of wanting and having. Believe and do your best. Leave the rest in God's hands.

Love with honesty and mortality. Remember that the core of Stoicism is virtue. When people enter into a relationship, they have the potential to create virtue and eventually to raise virtuous children. Relationships can then become a way to fulfill lust and live in a virtuous way. They can be warm and happy with couples living together virtuously and in harmony with nature.

THE PATHWAY TO SELF MASTERY

Human desires stem from our evolution. We evolved because of our innate desires for food, reproduction and aversion to discomfort in order to survive. Many of our basic instincts are shared with animals and in fact they have served us well. Overtime our desires have evolved for social hierarchy, sexual intercourse and more. It is this added combination of human creativity and imagination that has led our desires astray. Leading to unhealthy passions, compulsions and obsessions. In excess they have become dysfunctional and threaten our wellbeing. Desire can cause us unnecessary pain. Actualized this can be seen as a rational creature acting out of alignment with nature. Or more simply put a human acting as an animal.

In modern times advertising and marketing campaigns manipulate our desires to make us value and want things more. Our impulses are aroused to take advantage of our weaknesses for materialism, sex appeal, power and status. Stoicism was ahead of its times because they knew how easily humans could be led astray. They advocated that we need to constrain our human desire within reasonable boundaries. After all, their motto was to "live in alignment with nature." Now this doesn't mean to go back to our primal roots, nor to go and live in caves. Instead, it's about resisting desires which are excessive because going beyond your human natural limit often creates pain or conflict. Just take a look back through history and you will realize that many wars and conflicts were caused by people seeking more than what was necessary for their happiness.

Apatheia

Apatheia is the Stoic mindstate free from emotional disturbance. In literal terms it translates to living without passions. It is not to be confused with the word apathy which is a negative term. Apatheia is a positive term. Confusion between the two leads to detachment from reality. Apatheia helps us to effectively manage our emotions through recognizing and accepting them. According to Stoicism it is the fundamental purpose of humans to find Apatheia. Now please don't confuse that to mean living without emotions. Emotions and passions are different. Passions are the result of desire whilst emotions are part of the normal human experience. In those days the words also had a different meaning from our modern terminology. The ancient Stoics did not aim for a passionless life nor one without emotion. Self-awareness is the key. Even modern psychology tells us not to hide our emotions but to be aware of them. This is how we can make real changes and in turn live virtuously. Again, contrary to misjudgments Stoicism is not about depriving yourself. All of the emotions are experienced by them, but they choose to make the right choices not based on them but rather to be based on virtue.

Value comes from how you use it, not just to have it. Yes, we should have some things. For sure we need the essentials to live a comfortable life and we should always strive to improve our lives. We don't need to eliminate our desires completely. Commonly people come to Stoicism and assume they need to give up all their pleasures and vices. They think it will require them to give up things such as alcohol, drugs, sex and so on in the pursuit of happiness. They think that Stoicism forbids its followers from indulging in pleasures. Pleasure is not something we are forbidden from in Stoicism. No, you do not need to deprive yourself. We should still be inspired by beauty, to enjoy eating delicious food, to have fun with friends and so on.

A well-trained Stoic may for example may see someone attractive and feel a flicker of desire. Of course, this is a natural response. But that is not lust. Lust happens when someone imagines intimate relations with a person. They are consumed by the feeling and associate it as being good rather than what it really is which is indifferent. We think these things are inherently good but ultimately, they are indifferent. In the same regard our fear of missing out or fearing dispreferred things such as poverty, loneliness, low status and so on are also indifferent. All of these are based upon false beliefs appearing as real. Seneca the famous Stoic philosopher said we should enjoy the pleasures that come to us, but we must remain indifferent to their absence or presence.

In Stoicism, passions can be explained as giving assent to an impression. It is what comes after our automatic response to things. Those are beyond our control. This is the reasoning behind focusing on what is under our control. Freedom from our passions depends on releasing our emotional response to the events we don't control. Stoicism divides passions into healthy and unhealthy passions. A well-trained Stoic mind is able to know the difference. Ultimately, we need to learn to be happy with what we have. Be grateful and make the most of life. Focus on appreciating everything you have and cultivate having the right things. Not things to impress others or to distract us from our purpose.

Through Stoicism we can learn what truly makes us happy and realize how it affects us and what they truly are. A happy life involves pleasure, but it has to fit into the bigger picture and be clearly understood. Stoics state that you must follow virtue. Virtue is the guiding principle of Stoicism. It is the highest good and is a combination of the four qualities of wisdom, justice, courage and self-control. To truly experience pleasure, we must make virtue the ultimate pursuit. Through the pursuit of virtue, we will experience pleasure and happiness as by products. Make sure you follow that order of pursuit. Virtue is not something that can be faked. It is true and must be cultivated through real practice. If virtue is not there, then the pleasures of life will be hollow. They will control you and make you dependent on them.

Remember Stoicism is not a religion that promises damnation to those who fail its teachings. Following it is not a requirement. But if you do, your life will certainly improve. The Stoics knew that after all we are humans. We are not perfect. We will get tempted, attached, upset and we will fail.

All of that is fine. Realize, recognize and learn from it. Reflect on it and analyze how to improve because you have to be constantly improving. With an understanding of human nature, we can seek joy instead of pleasure. We can be cautious instead of fearful. We can wish for the best rather than to desire it. We can avoid grief, jealousy, depression, anguish, and worry. When we trust in the cosmic nature, we can love the outcome. This trust presents good in all events that occur no matter how bad they might seem. With this attitude we can grow and realize new opportunities. Through Stoicism one learns to love whatever happens to them because it is for the greater good of the universe. Life shapes us. Just like muscles are grown through discomfort. Consider your own challenges and how they have made you better. Ultimately this requires an assent to providence. Essentially that is to be guided by God.

"Wealth consists not in having great possessions, but in having few wants." –Epictetus

Discipline

Stoicism teaches us self-mastery through having self-control, responsibility, objectivity and self-examination. Without such discipline we would float through life and be at the whim of the world and our desires. Through discipline we can take charge of our lives. Whatever goals you have in life they will require work. Much of that work is about overcoming impulses and doing what's right even when you're tempted astray. Now that feeling of temptation doesn't necessarily disappear. But the more you act in spite of those impulses the stronger your discipline will become.

Epictetus said that we become free by removing desire not by filling our hearts with it. Longing or craving for something is a thing we share with animals, but we have the ability of reason to apply to our actions. Too many of us hope, crave and wish. We wish to meet the right partner, to lose weight and so on. But we often don't take enough action. We hold ourselves back. We can sit, pray and beg all we like but until we do something about it, our life will likely stay the same. Each of us has to take responsibility for ourselves, our thoughts and actions. Moving forward requires deliberate action. Not desire. It's ok to be intimidated by the obstacles you face. Don't wish for it to happen. Make it happen. Utilize discipline to overcome desires and take action.

Stoicism helps us to take the right course of actions and to have a strong willpower so that we do what is best for the universe. In the face of temptation this is useful because you're going to be tempted throughout life. Will you behave like an impulsive dog, or will you think before you act? Again, a Stoic is not someone lacking passion or emotion. They just know how to behave the right way. They know when enough is enough. As such they don't get lost in drugs, alcohol or addictions. Sure, they can indulge a little, but they know where the line is. That line is the difference between being controlled by something or being able to enjoy it on their own terms.

Discipline is one of the most important skills to mastering a successful life and overcoming unhealthy desires. When you master a part of your life it creates a positive feedback loop across the whole of your life. For example, getting your body in top form gives you more energy which leads to better productivity and business success. Or for example mastering your finances gives you more freedom to pursue your other goals. You get the picture. It's about mastering yourself so that you can live to your full potential. Always try your best at whatever you do. Never give less than one hundred percent. Often the reward is in the personal growth from the effort put in. Find what you're good at and go all in on it.

Many people think motivation is the key to getting things done. Indeed, it can get things done. Problem is that it comes and goes. Therefore, relying on it will not give you consistent results. That's where discipline comes in. When motivation is not there, discipline gets the job done. Realize that temptation and distraction make building discipline very hard. Emotions conflict with discipline because they affect our ability to resist temptation. In states of heightened emotions humans fail to be rational and they often engage in acts of immediate gratification, or they make bad decisions. Alcohol is a massive inhibitor here because it shuts down our logic. Ultimately the worst decisions are made when under the influence or when one is in a negative emotional state. In order to make it easier to be disciplined, identify and remove those inhibitors to your success. Avoid situations that cause temptation. If you're on a diet, get rid of junk food in your house. If you struggle with alcohol, then replace the feeling of a drink in your hand with a glass of soda. Most people usually just like having a drink in their hand. If you struggle with lust, block porn sites, track your compulsions and so on. Find out what your temptations are and work on ways to avoid them. Hide away the junk food, turn your phone on silent, work standing up and so on. Keep practicing discipline and give those muscles a workout. Excessive comfort diminishes discipline. Practice things which require discipline. For example, waking up early, cold showers, exercise, reading and so on. Start small and keep going. Stack the wins. What you feed grows. Feed your mind with discipline. Indeed, it can be difficult to cultivate more discipline because we have to be responsible for our actions.

Delayed gratification

Good things come to those who wait. This is one of the most important principles of building wealth or in fact anything worthwhile. Incidentally all religions promote delayed gratification as being one of the highest virtues of humans. They realize that humans who resist short term temptation will usually benefit in the long term. Sacrificing today will increase your quality of life in the future. I like to think of it as doing a favor for my future self. I thought of this every day when I set aside a year to work two jobs and invest in my business. Now I can live well thanks to my past sacrifices. Thanks to my friend in the past. Whilst those small sacrifices I make today will help me in the future. You save money to live a better retirement. Or you say no to the extra drink to save your morning and future health.

Delaying gratification is powerful because the benefits of it compound into the future. For example, you save money, and it continues to grow. You don't eat that cake, so you save your future health. We spend years studying and it can give us a lifetime of work and financial rewards. We invest in quality relationships, and they can improve our life infinitely. All of this makes our life infinitely better going forwards. Arguably it is one of the most important traits of a successful life. Therefore, all of us should learn and practice how to delay gratification. So how do we develop delayed gratification?

Realize that those who struggle with delayed gratification usually lack self-control and are controlled by their emotions. They struggle to resist temptation and it bites them back eventually. I have met so many people who didn't know where to draw the line. They always stayed up late and overindulged at parties. It negatively impacted their life. They lost their jobs and had to move back to their parents because they didn't know when to stop. They overindulged, overspent, overate and it messed up their futures. I have witnessed this over and over again. People left broke or dependent on their families because they didn't prepare for the future. Because they didn't know where to draw the line or understand the concept of delaying gratification. Recently we have witnessed this happen to millions of people who were not ready for the pandemic. People had gotten so used to living in the moment. Spending all they have and when the pandemic hit they were unprepared for it. Don't be like them! Learn how to delay gratification so that you can protect and promote your future. You will not be the one who goes out in a flash but instead someone who lives a long and prosperous life. Think of the turtle and the rabbit fable. The rabbit sprints the race and runs out of gas before the end. Meanwhile the turtle catches up at a slow pace and wins with ease.

Remind yourself of why you're delaying gratification. Usually, we focus on the immediate benefits but in order to stop doing those things that hurt us we need to look at the big picture. For example, if finance is a problem for you then create a compelling vision of the life you want to live. Set goals. In fact, set big goals that compel you. Choose a big goal in your life that means something to you. The things you want to achieve in this life, year, month, day and so on. Get clear on those and have a written account. Create that strong vision. Everyday feel, see and hear it. Creating a vision board of your goals can help you to manifest them. Find images that represent your goals. Look at them day and night. Feel them, see them and hear them. Always think in the big picture. Have a long-term vision of success beyond immediate gratification? This will help you through the ups and the downs. Think of it like your stock market portfolio and watch it grow over the years. We should always be working towards something because it will keep us focused and driven towards succeeding. Stay accountable also by having someone to keep track of your challenges, achievements and so on. This will help you to build confidence and more resilience as you go onwards and upwards.

HOW TO MASTER & CONTROL YOUR EMOTIONS

Stoicism is often misjudged as the suppression of emotions. Really this is not true. Much like other humans, Stoics feel all of the emotions. Contrary to popular belief Stoicism does not advocate the absence of emotions. Instead, what it teaches is to gain mastery of our emotions so that we are not carried away by them. One will never be free from negative emotions, but one can learn to gain control over them. This isn't about denying or suppressing your natural emotions. No, it's about understanding those emotions and coming up with the most effective responses. To be free from false judgments and to align with the truth that sets you free. In turn this will make you an all-round, happier, and better human.

According to Stoicism emotions are the excessive attachment to preferred indifferents. Emotions influence our approach to different situations. Each of us has our own unique emotional character. Optimistic people tend to make optimistic decisions whilst pessimists tend to make pessimistic decisions. The glass is either half full or half empty. Essentially, we view things in different ways based on our own unique emotional characteristics. Most of this is unconscious and that can cloud our rational judgment. Appetite, fear, pleasure and distress are the four main types of emotion. Fear and appetite are faulty judgements of things being good or bad. Whilst distress and pleasure are faulty judgements of things in the present. Within each of these are subcategories.

- Fear - the expectation of something bad happening. The soul shrinks and we experience agony, hesitation, dread, panic and terror.
- Distress - an irrational shrinking of the soul and the experience of emotions such as envy, malice, grief, pity, anguish, annoyance and so on.
- Appetite - when the soul irrationally stretches or swells in expectation of something good such as wanting, anger, craving, yearning and so on.
- Pleasure - heightened feelings towards what seems

worthy such as self-gratification, rejoicing over another misfortune, enchantment and so on.

Emotions are powerful. They can cloud your judgment and cause you to act wrongly or to make mistakes. Just think back to your past. I'm sure you can recount many times where you got angry and said or did the wrong thing. Or maybe you misread a situation when your emotions led you astray. Losing control of your emotions often causes much more long term hurt. Recently I witnessed an enraged man kick and punch another person's car. Is that helping anyone? To me it looked like the behavior of a child. Such behavior could have landed him a night in jail or a big fine. Tantrums will not get us what we want in life. Realistically they are an immature management of emotions.

All of us have at one time or another done or said something foolish because of our emotional response. You get angry at the waiter for bringing food late. You get lazy and leave things to the last minute. It is these emotions that can cloud our rational minds. We like to think we are rational but for the most part we are not. Emotions are a subjective state of mind. They come from our bodily reactions to a stimulus and then we feel them in our heads. Fear makes us sweat and shake. Love makes our hearts beat faster.

Our body registers an emotion first and therefore it is not possible for us to use conscious powers to stop emotions. However, we can use our conscious power to redirect our emotional states. After experiencing an uncomfortable reaction, we can control how we respond consciously to be better for the mutual benefit of the universe. This method is at the heart of many psychiatric therapies such as cognitive behavioral therapy in addition to ancient philosophies, like Buddhism. In an ideal world a person makes their rational decisions with little disturbance from emotions. For example, it rains and that changes your plans. Or you get stuck in traffic, and it makes you late. How would you react? With anger? With frustration? Or would you act like a Stoic? A Stoic would not let their initial impressions carry them away. They would try to be objective and in turn choose the best response.

Mastery of your emotions will enable you to do the right thing even in the face of adversity. Stillness can be found in chaos with tranquility of mind regardless of the external situation. Imagine the commander in a war zone who must stay calm and not be overtaken by emotions. Otherwise, it would be catastrophic. Stoicism helps one to be more emotionally resilient in adversity. It offers the student a new way of viewing the world, a framework to manage it through and a philosophy for life. Emotional resilience is about being able to deal with stress without being overwhelmed by it. When we are faced with obstacles and challenges, we often become emotional. But the best way to overcome them is to keep our emotions in check and stay grounded. In staying grounded we are better prepared for the fluctuations of life. This is something we can all work on making stronger. Stoicism is synonymous with this mindset.

Stimulus, Perception & Response

When misfortune hits us, it can be difficult not to be swept away by autopilot reactions. Seneca taught that it is the unexpected challenges of life which are the most difficult to ascertain control over. However, there is a gap between when we experience something and our judgment of it. When something happens, you have the opportunity to pause and consider how you judge it and then to decide how to respond. For example, when someone gossips about you, initially it can cause shock or upset. Either you can choose to let that settle into resentment or you can choose to move on. Or for example when someone cuts you off in traffic. Naturally this angers most people. But you can choose to be overwhelmed by the feeling of anger or to let it pass.

Ultimately, we have the power of choice over our thoughts and actions. Of course, doing the right thing requires practice. Practicing Stoicism can help us to improve our thoughts. But it often takes many years. Recognize the power of your thoughts because they are what create your world. Literally they can change your physiology and external world. The ancient Stoics were well aware of the power of thought. They recognized we have the power to respond how we want. If you experience rejection, do you take it personally or do you take it as a learning curve? If your team wins or loses, do you get depressed or do you let it go? Remember it is you who has the choice.

Epictetus said that thought was the first step in how humans become upset or stressed. We make judgments of things as being either bad or good. Sometimes these judgments can be extreme. When you get angry at someone you are judging something they did as being bad. But it doesn't need to be that way. After thought comes impulse. This is the impulse to act in an automatic way. For example, shouting when we are angry. Epictetus uses the term differently. Instead, he says that impulses are the first step as to when we judge something as being good, bad or indifferent. Essentially, they are our value judgments or our desire to act. We judge things all the time and make decisions on how to act. All day, every day this happens, both quickly and slowly.

According to Stoicism there are three stages of emotion:

1. Stimulus: An experience that could be coming from the outside, people or even your internal thoughts. The thought itself, without endorsement - which is the appearance of emotion. We can make use of the discipline of desire here.

2. Perception: Assent or endorsement of the thought - this is our power to apply rational and take control of our emotions. Inside your mind the stimulus is processed. How you perceive it depends on your thoughts, beliefs and values. We can make use of the discipline of assent here.

3. Response: How you choose to respond. This also depends on your thoughts, beliefs and values. We can make use of the discipline of action here.

Stimulus & The Discipline of Desire

Biologically as humans we were all designed the same in the ways to which we react to stimulus. From the day we were born we have had primitive emotional programs that help to ensure our survival. As we grow our brain evolves to understand the patterns that threaten our survival. When a perceived threat is detected, an automatic response is initiated. This happens not just with threats but in a variety of situations. Through nature and nurture, we develop automatic responses. These are largely unconscious and oftentimes in the modern world they don't help us so much. Do not feel guilty for your initial feelings because they are involuntary. The Stoics called this "propatheiai", and it is completely normal. Think of it as nature's way of keeping us from harm.

Our initial impressions of stimuli are not subject to any discipline because we cannot control the impressions that present themselves to us. Only when we respond to those impressions is when we become responsible for them. For most of us we attempt to handle things at the last stage, which is the impulse to act. We see some delicious food, an attractive person, an expensive suit and so on. This is presented to us as being of value and we assent to triggering desire for it. Some of us may even fantasize over having it. In the end we want it more and this makes us act on our impulses.

Wise people are indeed also gripped by initial events as part of the human experience. There is no shame in that. But they look at what can be done and ask themself questions such as, is it really that bad? Or what can I do to improve it? We can make use of this process in various situations such as moments of danger, anger, shock, fear and so on. Essentially in the moments that cause sudden involuntary reactions. Allow yourself to first feel that initial primal instinct. Accept it and then make a conscious effort to see it objectively. Let me elaborate through a story.

Once upon a time a Stoic philosopher took his students to sail across the seas. Rough waves and weather rocked the boat violently on its journey. The men and women on board panicked at the fear of it sinking. In the moment the Stoic philosopher was also gripped by fear. He remained silent in the face of the storm. After the storm had passed one of the students asked the Stoic why he was afraid. Surely, he as a Stoic would be able to handle the fear. He responded that even a wise man is disturbed by terror and danger. However, he does not hold onto those emotions. Ultimately, he realizes they are indifferent. The fool on the other hand is also overwhelmed by the fear but he yields to it. Whilst the wise man stays steadfast and acts appropriately and rationally. Even though he feels fear just the same as the fool he does not let the terror excite him or cause him to make a bad judgement. This treatment is true with all emotions in Stoicism.

The discipline of desire helps us to not let things spiral out of control. Practicing the discipline of desire requires the cardinal virtues of temperance and courage. One must as Epictetus says, "endure and renounce". Through practice we can avoid irrational pleasures and aversions that in the short term feel good but in the long term hurt us. In order to practice the discipline of desire we must continue to live in alignment with universal nature as a whole. One must also accept their fate as inevitable. We talked about this earlier "Amor Fati" which is to love the acceptance of one's fate. Caro of Utica, a famous Stoic hero exemplifies this. Through the deserts of Africa, he marched in an attempt to overthrow Julius Caesar. In the end he lost the civil war but became a legend because rather than submit to Julius Caesar he pulled out his own guts with his bare hands.

"Seek not for events to happen as you wish but wish events to happen as they do and your life will go smoothly and serenely." - Enchiridion

Perception & The Discipline of Assent

From impulse comes a second response which is our conscious response. Remember that the wise man and the fool are separated by the space between stimulus and response. The fool is overcome by the stimulus and lacks the rationale to respond in the correct way. Whilst the wise man is able to look at it objectively which is what the discipline of assent is about. Essentially it is awareness of your inner world. Think of it like mindfulness.

Notice that you make value judgments all the time. Our judgments influence the way we view the world around us. Of paramount importance to Stoics is the assessment of good or bad judgments. We associate value to various things when often they are indifferent to us. Essentially the labels we associate with external events and people are that way because we chose them to be. Yet labeling them is not necessary. In Stoicism everything is seen as an opportunity. There is no good or bad but only perception. So, what exactly is perception? In simple terms it is how one sees a situation or interprets and understands it. However, that often is not a true reflection of reality. For example, someone who was lied to by a man in a previous relationship might now perceive all men as being liars. But this just is not true reality. Indeed, there are some men who are liars but not all of them are.

When we make value judgments all too often, they are overly emotional because we are using emotional terminology. Don't allow yourself to do this. Instead try to describe the situation in a more factual and logical way. For example, instead of saying you missed your flight and describing how awful it was. Instead, you could say, I missed my flight and now I am booking a new one. Avoiding emotional language to describe the situation will help you to worry less and to be less overwhelmed by it. After all you cannot change what has happened, but you can change how it affects you.

Realize that those emotions and judgments come from your own internal creations. Nothing really needs to be perceived as being bad or even good. Ultimately that perception is your own choice. Stoicism teaches us to stop adding those value judgments so that we can think more accurately and clearly. Think of it as non-judgmental awareness to see the world exactly for what it is without distortion. Allow yourself to create a space between impression and judgment.

One must see things the way they truly are and be mindful of when they are thinking because it is the gateway to controlling one's thoughts and emotions. View the world in an objective way without clouding it with judgment or lies to oneself. Self-awareness is crucial to ensure correct judgements and actions. Continually work on becoming more self-aware. Practice makes perfect. Through consistent internal monitoring one can apprehend in advance any early warning signs of unhealthy impressions or desires which could cause going against one's nature. With this in mind, we can remain self-aware, calm and rational regardless of circumstances. Remember to focus on what you control, which is your emotions and actions. Everything else is going to play out as it will. Keep rolling with the punches and bouncing back stronger. Through practicing Stoicism one can improve their perceptions which in turn leads to a happier and healthier life.

"Do not seek for things to happen the way you want them to; rather, wish that what happens, happens the way it happens: then you will be happy." - Epictetus

Response & The Discipline of Action

Stoicism teaches us that we must be responsible for the way in which we respond to the world. Humans naturally learn behaviors from nature and nurture which form a pattern of responses. As a result, we frequently end up making automatic responses to situations based on our behaviors. Incidentally while it might seem optimal, not all of this automation helps us. Early Stoic philosophers were well aware of patterned behaviors and responses. To counter them they practiced self-awareness so that they could be more critical in their perceptions and opinions.

How you respond is ultimately your choice and this depends on your beliefs and character. Becoming aware of how you respond is very important because if it is left alone then destructive patterns can begin to form. Think of it like a house you need to clean every so often. We can get lost in life and go through the motions. Take time to reflect on how you respond to situations. Could you improve upon those responses? Maybe you responded angrily to a challenge. Maybe you misinterpreted a relationship and missed out on a great opportunity. Analyze and reflect on your triggers. Work on cultivating better responses.

When we change our beliefs, we can change our responses. Perhaps that's about being more open minded or less attached to an outcome. Align with cosmic nature, understand and accept your choice as a human. As the dichotomy of control states, there are things which we have within our control and things which are not. Within our control are our own internal choices, desires, aversions, motivations and opinions. Whilst outside of our control are the material, reputations and things not of our own doing.

The discipline of action is about harmonious living with all mankind and wishing them the best. Even when others may not wish the best for you. Ultimately you cannot control them, but you can control your own responses and actions. It is in your power of choice to act virtuously and to help others. When someone acts angrily you don't need to respond the same way they did or even to be offended by them. Simply accept who they are and don't let it affect you. Do your best to act with virtue and accept the actions of others with detachment. A good Stoic does their best to act virtuously whilst accepting they cannot control outcomes of their actions. Act purposefully with virtue.

SHARPENING THE SWORD

Every day we are faced with obstacles that can overwhelm our emotions. Things take us by surprise, people can challenge and confront us. Indeed, life sucks sometimes and things often go wrong. We all experience it and there is no way around this. However, too many of us are ignorant and oblivious of this fact. We think catastrophe would never happen to us. But when it comes along, we are destroyed by it.

In a letter to his friend Lucilius Seneca answered the question, why do many evils happen to good people? Seneca replied that the Gods who control the universe have a friendship with us. The Gods challenge us with trials to make us stronger. Seneca also goes on to say that there is no bad thing for a good person. A brave person stays balanced in the face of adversity; it hardly affects them. Strong people pick challenging circumstances to make themselves better. To sharpen their sword so to say. Seneca challenges his friend to stay prosperous throughout life without any mental distress. To stay calm in the face of challenge and adversity.

"He who has waged an unceasing strife with his misfortunes has gained a thicker skin by his sufferings" - Seneca

Ultimately everything is temporary. Throughout history people have overcome adversity and gone on to inspire the world. Muhammad Ali became champion of the world whilst faced with racism and being stripped of his titles. The world overcame tyrants in World War Two. Marcus Aurelius faced numerous invasions, plagues and adversities. There are so many countless examples from history. All of these people who faced adversity no doubt felt fear, depression and overwhelming negative emotions. Yet they stood up and thrived despite that. Stoicism can help us to do the same.

First of all, we have to realize that perception is the key. The way we perceive and understand what happens to us and the world around us makes a huge difference in our quality of life. We decide what our perception and understanding is. This can either hold us back or lift us up. Stoicism teaches us to see the external as neither good nor bad but as indifferent. Therefore, it is our judgment of the indifferent which matters to us. It is you who must take responsibility for your judgment.

There is what happens to us and the story we tell ourselves about the meaning. How you perceive different situations will determine how you feel about them. Consequently, this will influence the ways in which you act. When you feel it's impossible you give up? But when you feel it's tough but manageable then you keep on going. Try taking yourself out of the equation. Get a birds eye view on it and make an objective rational decision. Realize that you have the power in your hands. Even though circumstances may be out of your control we can still control ourselves, the ways we think, our attitude, efforts and so on.

The Toxic Emotion of Stress

Zeno the founder of Stoicism lost everything he had in a shipwreck. Seneca was exiled and suffered numerous health problems. Marcus Aurelius reigned over an empire during plagues, wars, bankruptcy, flooding and numerous other problems. Epictetus was a slave for thirty years. Such stresses they all faced. Stress comes from hard times, uncertainty, failure and pain. All of which are a part of everyday life. All of us face stress but that doesn't mean we have to be stressed by it. Sometimes it can become so overwhelming and there is not much you can do about that. Except the way you decide on how to deal with it.

Marcus Aureilius chose not to feel harmed. He talked about releasing and discarding stress. His journals were filled with notes on escaping stress and learning not to let anger control him. Epictetus repeatedly taught his students to focus on what was in their control and to let go of everything else. Stress relief at its finest! Seneca wrote not to suffer before it is necessary, and that stress is optional. Even though we are being stressed we don't need to let it overwhelm us.

According to Stoicism stress is a reaction to our perception. We feel stressed when our perception fails to meet our expectations. The point is that all too often we suffer more in imagination than in reality. We worry about how bad things will be. We all go through tough times, and you can't escape that fact. But we don't need to suffer so much from thoughts of pain that never happened. When you for example have an injury, pain comes from the damage inflicted. But more suffering comes from the thoughts about it. Such thoughts are not facts, they are just thoughts in your head. True you are in pain, but you don't need to create vivid stories about it or wallow in unnecessary self-pity.

As Seneca advises "do not be unhappy before the crisis comes." When you feel stressed out, analyze the feeling. Where does it come from? Dissect it. Consider whether you are bringing it on yourself. Cut it out before it grows. Adjust your expectations. When we expect too much it can leave us frustrated. Instead work on having more appropriate expectations. The more realistic they are, the better your experience will be. Furthermore, Epictetus said our main task in life is to identify and separate what one controls and what they do not. When you let go of worrying about what is not in your control it frees up your time and energy onto what you can. This gives you a distinct advantage in stressful situations. When we are being more responsible and creative, stress is going to be reduced.

"You have power over your mind not outside events, realize this and you will find strength." - Seneca

When we change our perception of our environment, we can see the bigger picture which reduces our stress. Those small conflicts, disagreements and arguments seem so small in the grand scheme of things. When troubles come to you, stay focused on the bigger picture. Often what you think is a big deal is a small thing. Zoom out and see it on a grand scale of your life in the world. The View from Above is an exercise which the ancient Stoics practiced visualizing how we are all connected through the universe. One imagines oneself high up in space looking down at planet Earth below. This shifts their point of view from a first person to a third person perspective. Essentially this is a psychological process known as cognitive distancing which involves separating your thoughts for yourself. Writing your thoughts down is another great way to do this because it brings thoughts out of your head and into the world. Again, this creates distance and separates us from them.

Try looking at yourself in the third person view. Reflect on your problems as a third person. For example, John is thinking..., as if you are studying them. Shifting your perspective will help you to free up your thinking. Furthermore, you could also imagine how other people would deal with your thoughts. For example, what would Seneca do?

Laugh often

Apparently, a famous Stoics, Chrysippus, died from laughing. What a way to go! The ancient Stoics believed humor was essential to living in a world marked with suffering and challenges. They believed we should have a lighter view of things so that we can easily move through the world. Science proves that laughter and humor release the happy chemicals of endorphins in the brain. Instead of being so serious, look on the bright side and find the humor in things. Cultivate your inputs. Stop watching so many shows and movies. Switch to something more lighthearted. Watch funny shows, make jokes and find humor in every situation. After all, it will keep you happy and youthful.

"He who laughs has joy. The very soul must be happy and confident, lifted above every circumstance." - Seneca

See obstacles as opportunities

The ancient Stoics believed that within every obstacle was an opportunity. Regardless of how bad a situation may seem there is always an opportunity there. It could be a lesson to learn, just look for it. Every time you face an obstacle see it as an opportunity. Too many of us think of obstacles as preventing our happiness and stopping our pursuit of our goals. But instead, we can reframe them to be challenges. For example, when you get stuck in traffic see it as an opportunity to cultivate more patience. Or when you face setbacks see them as an opportunity to become stronger and more persistent.

Our world is always changing. We need to be ready for change. Ultimately, we have little control over what happens to us. However, we can decide upon our reaction to it. Maybe you adopt the mindstate of a victim. You think, why did this happen to me? Instead, why not look for the opportunity? There is a famous story of a farmer whose son fell from a horse and broke his leg. People go on to say to the farmer such things as, "that must be so terrible". "Maybe" he replies. Soon after a war breaks out and all the young men are enlisted. Except his son because he is injured. Maybe it wasn't so terrible after all.

The next time you're challenged, try to apply the same way of thinking. What is the value in this? How is this good? Ultimately good can be found in any situation. Sometimes that means turning things upside down. A potentially bad situation becomes good and so on. For example, you were late for an appointment but maybe you missed something negative happening to you. Or someone is mean to you and things don't go your way. Maybe they are teaching you knew values or helping you to improve.

The only reason difficult situations become obstacles is because we choose to make them that way. Instead, we need to look at them in a new way. A way that envisions progress and opportunity. We have the choice to be blocked by challenges or to fight. To shrink or to grow. Ultimately this comes down to our perception. If your glass is half full or half empty? It is not about being naive to the bad things that happen. Yes, they do happen, but we should not bury our heads in the sand. We should fight and keep going. Train your perceptions to look for opportunities. See adversity as a chance to grow and test you. Seek goals and challenges that will test and improve you. Remember to have no expectation or attachment to the outcome.

Mindfulness

Most stress comes from when the mind wanders to a place other than the present moment. When it latches onto fear of the future, regret of the past or gets lost in thought. Practice being mindful. Being mindful of emotions will help you to understand if they are helpful or not. Furthermore, this will help you to choose the best actions of virtue.

The present moment is all we have. Time continues to move and can never be pinpointed. When you try to pinpoint it it becomes the past or the future. Neither exist yet all too often we try to live there. In doing so we sacrifice the present moment which is the only place we can truly live in. Living in alignment with nature requires us to live in the present. Keep yourself in the present moment and enjoy life to the fullest. The present moment is your life happening right now. Don't miss out on it. Work on cultivating mindfulness through exercises such as yoga or meditation. Both of these focus on connecting with the present moment through breathing or mantras. Take time out each and every day to practice. Learn more about them through YouTube, courses, books, workshops and home practice.

The Toxic Emotion of Anger

Seneca famously called anger "a temporary madness". In that state a person becomes unreasonable and lacks rational. Anger can quickly erupt like a volcano exploding, boiling over and creating chaos. It spreads like wildfire in people which is unique since emotions are rarely so contagious and collective. Populations, companies, teams and collectives can become infected with anger. Imagine mob behavior when people work together in violence, chaos and disruption. Seemingly normal people wouldn't do such crazy things alone. Yet together they cause havoc.

Emotionally it is one of the most intense feelings. One becomes almost unconscious under its spell. We often get angry over such trivial things. The traffic, the weather, the spilled milk. Instead, realize that getting angry only makes things worse because we end up hurting ourselves or others more than the event itself. Anger takes us over and distorts us. It turns the calm into a raging monster. Our ability to reason is clouded when we are angry. This leads us to make bad decisions and actions. We are not being our normal rational self. As a result of this we end up doing more harm than what the anger caused. Someone gets cut off in traffic and they become violent. Or an argument rises into regretful things said. All of us are affected by it regardless of background or personality type. Even the most gentle and peaceful people can be affected. In those moments of anger, we are blinded by the future consequences of our angry actions. We make bad decisions, behave recklessly and cause much more damage than the anger did.

The ancient Stoics studied anger in depth. They understood that it can be prevented once one realizes the faults of anger. First of all, realize that anger inflicts harm. Harm to yourself and harm to others. For those who think that anger makes them stronger then really, they are trapped by it. When we become angry, we become a slave of it because it makes us blind and causes us to make mistakes which we will likely later regret. Just think of those times when you got angry. You probably did or said something you now regret. The majority of road accidents occur when people are angry. People are hurt, murdered and killed because of anger. How much of this could have been avoided if people learned to let go of anger? How many lives could be saved? Or wars avoided?

Working towards an anger free life requires a tranquil mind. This should be your highest goal. Once you realize how destructive anger is you can work towards breaking attachment to it. That's the start of your journey. Understand that anger is not beneficial. It won't help you or anyone else. In fact, it will only make things worse than what initially made you angry. Tranquility is a better strategy. Realize that civilness and gentleness are more human traits.

Now if you consider yourself to be someone who has a hot temper then learn what triggers it and find ways to soothe it. Being mindful and taking notes will help you here. The next time you feel yourself getting angry. Ask yourself why. What caused it? Make a note of that mentally, verbally or write it down. Moving forward, try to avoid those situations that often make you angry. For example, if you see a que of people then come back later. If the news makes you angry, then avoid it.

Furthermore, make use of specific practices to calm the mind. Listen to music that is calming, go for walks to unwind. Have a workout routine to destress or meditate. Get lost in an art gallery. Set aside times for these periods where you practice calmness and letting go. We can weaken anger by consciously being aware of the costs of it. Don't let the small things arouse anger. Try to stay calm even in the midst of the storms. Cultivate this mindset through experience. Become aware of those things that usually make you angry and try to stay calm during those times.

"Anger, if not restrained, is frequently more hurtful to us than the injury that provokes it" - Seneca

Here are some more points of wisdom from Seneca on dealing with anger:

Let time pass

Seneca advised that the greatest solution for anger was to let time pass so that the initial passion could die down. Simply waiting for some time to pass is a great way to calm the flames of anger. Emotions are transient and never last forever. Knowing this we can simply wait for anger to pass. Time and distance are the best solutions. The further away we are from anger the stronger we become. Interrupt the pathway of anger with time. Take fifty deep breaths, count to one hundred backwards or repeat the alphabet during those times.

See yourself as the offender

Seneca advises that we see ourselves as the offender in angry confrontations with others. When you get angry with someone, visualize yourself as them. Put yourself in their position. Is your anger still justified? Would you put up with how you're treating them? Is it acceptable behavior on your part? When you flip the script onto yourself the anger will quickly subside, and you can determine the correct way to proceed since you are coming from a mindset which is not clouded. Furthermore, if you have empathy for others, it will make you more tolerant of them. Maybe they are young or inexperienced. No one is perfect. All of us have our own flaws. Perhaps you have made the same mistakes before.

Marcus Aureilis took the view that everyone was doing their best and that they don't have ill will for others. The more tolerance you develop the more you can deal with personal conflicts. However, in developing tolerance it is important to not let people cross your boundaries or to take advantage of you. Always maintain healthy boundaries but at the same time have a higher threshold for not getting angry. All of this comes through experience. Staying calm when everyone else gets mad. When things go wrong it helps you continue to make good decisions which are not clouded by anger.

When we are hurt or wronged, we often want to take revenge. Prisons are based on this concept. Punishment for wrongdoing. However, people often come out of prison and offend again. Progressive countries are starting to look at ways to heal rather than to punish. Now I'm not saying we should let people go without paying for the consequences of their actions. But the more we can let go of seeking revenge the better we can establish ourselves away from anger which fuels revenge. Seneca said that vengeance takes time and can expose one to more injuries and resentment. Catch yourself when you get caught up in that rage of revenge. Try to see the person in the whole picture. For whom they are. For what kind of character, they have. Everyone makes mistakes.

Remember to choose your friends carefully because anger is highly contagious. We become the average of people we associate with. If you're associating with negative angry people, then that will influence your behavior. It can be all too easy to be led astray and you don't want to get caught up in a mob. After all, you're only human. Cultivate relationships with people who are calm, honest, positive, tranquil and who have good self-control.

Question you thoughts

We can easily get carried away by our thoughts. Therefore, we have to question if those thoughts are rational and true. Seneca suggests that we do battle with ourselves. When you have the will to conquer anger it will become difficult for it to conquer you. Smile in the face of anger. Relax yourself and question it. Fight against the bodily movements and thought patterns of anger. Switch them to being calmer and happier.

Your opinion about something is what upsets you. Not the behaviors or the people. How much you value something determines the level of anger that comes from it. Think about it. Do you get upset by the same behaviors when it occurs in different contexts? For example, people being late. Or getting wet in the rain. Bear these value judgements in mind. Question whether they are really that important? Furthermore, question whether or not they are in your control.

Through self-reflection you can realize your ways of thinking and triggers for negative emotions. Practice some daily self-reflection to get in tune with what causes you anger and learn to slow it down. Seneca was a big advocate of self-reflection. He taught that our senses should be trained to make us stronger and durable. Marcus Aurelius understood that we should be aware of the circumstances which cause anger. Both would agree that we should reject anger and not be carried away by it. Like an enemy it must be met and driven back.

"Holding onto anger is like drinking poison and expecting the other person to die" - Seneca

The Toxic Emotion of Jealousy

Through the eyes of Stoicism jealousy is an illusion of permanence combined with believing that the external will make us happy. Realize that the universe is impermanent and that the external is outside of our control. When one is jealous, they wish not to lose something external and as such they attach themselves to it. Epictetus taught that we never own what we are attached to. The presence of it is temporary in our lives and in the blink of an eye we could lose it all. Understand that nothing lasts forever because one day you will ultimately be separated from it.

Now that doesn't mean you should be alone and have nothing

to live for. Marcus Aurelius wrote that we shouldn't set our minds on what we don't possess. Instead, we ought to count our blessings for what we have and consider how much we might desire them if we didn't have them. Essentially, it's about making the most of what you have whilst you have it. Life changes constantly and change is the only constant. Resisting change makes us insecure. Jealousy arises from insecurity. We can never predict change, so it makes no sense to worry about trying to influence it or to worry about its influences. We can only do our best in this moment. The rest we have to embrace. Amor Fati reminds us to embrace and to love our fate.

Ultimately, we could put all of our efforts into relationships, status and possessions. But we can still lose them in an instant because ultimately you cannot truly control such externalities. In addition, they are also indifferents. Preferred indifferents that is but also still indifferent which means they aren't essential to happiness. True happiness can be found in virtue which is to be free and not moved by misfortune. Stop focusing on the external and switch your focus to the internal. Obsession over anything will eventually push it away from you. Live abundantly and freely. Incidentally when you focus on living in abundance instead of anxiety and clinging you will inevitably attract more people, moments and greatness into your life.

"Count the blessings you actually possess and think how much you would desire them if they weren't already yours."
– Marcus Aurelius

The Toxic Emotion of Envy

Envy comes from social comparison. In our modern world we are surrounded by highlights of people being happy. Social media shows us just that, the highlights of someone's life. Naturally we assume that our life should be just as awesome. However, in reality, life is not a series of highlights. There is pain, struggle and a journey behind any life. All of which contribute to our growth and potential to become better. Chasing fleeting highlights will only lead to disappointment and guilt when you fall short of them.

Everyone has their own fortunes and starting points in life. Therefore, it is worthless to compare yourself to them or to be envious of them. But all too often we define ourselves in comparison to others. This is a powerful influence in how we conceptualize our own worth. When we feel inferior in some way you value whether it be beauty, wealth or so on then envy comes in. Ultimately envy is a reflection about how we feel about ourselves. When we are not smart enough, fit enough or beautiful enough and so on. Yet all of these are preferred indifferents and they are not in our control. Furthermore, they are impermanent and could disappear in an instant.

Lose your ego. Ego is a distorted view of one's significance and abilities. It is an unhealthy belief in how important one is. Ego leads to arrogance, recklessness and stubbornness. It stands in the way of what you want and could have. The ego is focused on being better than others. Don't focus on them. Focus on being your best. Stop comparing and showing off. Live your life and be your best. Live a life of virtue. Work without desire for recognition. The more you work against the ego the more it diminishes. Eventually you become more aligned with nature.

Envy is a poison of the mind. It puts a barrier between others and pushes you away from real connection with people. When people cling to thoughts of envy it causes them to practice immoral behaviors such as infidelity and criminal acts. But envy is not all bad. In fact, we can utilize it to improve ourselves as an inspiration to improve weaknesses. Think about some of your idols or inspirational things you have watched. Those probably make you feel small, but they also inspire you to become bigger and better.

So how does one overcome envy? First of all it requires self-awareness and examination. Become aware of your envy. Ask yourself why you are envious. Can you justify it? If you are envious of another person, realize that we all have different advantages at stages of life. The pathway through envy is in being grateful for what you have. Focus on what you have and make it better. That way you can only ever compare yourself to who you used to be and who you are now. Instead of always seeking external validation and satisfaction look inwards. Realize that happiness is created from within your own mind. Outside events do not create it.

Stoicism can help you here to focus on what you have. It teaches us to be mindful of the present. To let go of energy spent living in the past or worrying about the future. Happiness and peace of mind come from within. They do not depend on the opinions of other people; they are all too important to give power over to someone else. Life is too short for that. Embrace the person you are and what makes you unique. Stop caring what others think. Go for what you want and be ruthless. Stop trying to please people and be someone you're not. Be you. In the cases where we desire something internal such as inner peace or happiness then it's a sign, we need to work more on ourselves. Pursuing virtue helps us to become stronger and to vanquish envy.

Marcus Aurelius the famous Stoic emperor wrote negatively about validation seeking behavior. This is enlightening for someone who would have been so famous in his time to write about. These days people are constantly seeking validation. Social media is prevalent and all about this. It has made the world imbalanced. People are praised for meaningless accomplishments and are gratified by likes, comments or follows. All this activates our dopamine happiness secreting chemicals which gives us temporary hits of pleasure. On the other hand, if we don't get it then we feel sad. Too many people are addicted to those hits and spend their lives chasing them. Whilst the world of love, joy and real social connections continue outside of their online bubble. Remember again that all of this is out of our control. With the rise of online connections, we are open to being viewed by much more people and judged by much more people. Maintain the same attitude of not caring what they think. Now that doesn't mean being arrogant. On the contrary you still act your best self and be a kind person but at the same time you let go of what people think of you. Face it not everyone will like you. No matter how much you try, some people just don't like you. Choose not to be hurt by the opinions of others. Choose to focus on your own mental wellbeing and be proud of who you are.

"Ambition means tying your well-being to what other people say or do...Sanity means tying it to your own actions." - Marcus Aurelius

THE POWER OF NEGATIVE THINKING

The modern self-help industry tells us to think positively, encouraging us to be happy all day and to ignore any negative emotions. But without acknowledging pains and the negative emotions underlying then we are just glossing over deeper problems. Some studies have even shown that avoiding negative emotions only makes them stronger which can lead to more stress later on. Essentially in avoiding negative emotions you are being dishonest with yourself. Often from places of pain, darkness and struggle is where we grow the most.

When we are comfortable with expressing negative emotions, it will help us become more comfortable with who we are. We can learn to understand ourselves better and have a deeper, true self love. Failure to recognize negative emotions or to pacify them with escape behaviors will never resolve the underlying problems. In fact, numerous studies have proven that the expression of negative emotions helps to build strong relationships. Don't escape and pacify your hurt with vices such as junk food or escapism. Give yourself some time out now and then but over the long-term focus on small daily improvements to dig yourself out of that hole and become your best self.

"A gem cannot be polished without friction, nor a man perfected without trials." – Seneca

Premeditatio Malorum

Stoicism encourages us to expect that things will go wrong sometimes. Premeditatio Malorum or "the premeditation of evils" is a mental exercise taught in Stoicism to help students imagine the worst possible scenarios of what could happen to them. According to Stoicism we should be ready for challenges and adversity. They are inevitable and so we should consider everything that could possibly go wrong. Think about it. What are the challenges you could face and what would you do about them? Those who can thrive in the hard times are able to do so by focusing on what they can control to make the situation better. Seneca believed that by doing this exercise he would be prepared for any fate that he might meet with. Incidentally he faced many adversities in his life including being exiled as a prisoner for many years. Through each adversity he persevered with strength, bravery and understanding. Victory and defeat he dealt with equally.

The goal of Premeditatio Malorum is to help one prepare for life's adversities and uncertainties because things won't always go to plan as we hope. Therefore, we need to build a strong psychological foundation to help prepare us for when things go wrong. The more we prepare the further we can go. Positive thinking will get you started but you also need some cynicism to ensure you go all the way. For example, think of what it takes to start a business. If you were overly optimistic you might run out of cash too soon. However, with a bit of Premeditatio Malorum you would realize that running out of money is likely to happen. As such you would prepare accordingly and be able to run through any dip that might happen. Furthermore, if it doesn't happen more strength to you!

"Rehearse them in your mind: exile, torture, war, shipwreck. All the terms of our human lot should be before

our eyes." - Seneca

Consider any goal or upcoming event you have in mind and apply this strategy to it. What's the worst that could happen? How would you overcome that? Your answers should give you some clear-cut plans in the event of any tragedy occurring. Now hopefully that doesn't happen but, in any case, you should be prepared. Tim Ferriss, the bestselling author came up with his own version of Premeditatio Malorum and he called it "fear setting". There are four steps to fear setting.

- Step one: Write down whatever it is you are not confident about doing. Maybe that is applying for a new job, going on a date or traveling to a new place.
- Step two: Write down what your worries of things that could go wrong are. Maybe you could get a rejection. Maybe things don't go to plan, or you screw up.
- Step three: Write down what you would do if these worst-case scenarios actually happened. How would you overcome them?
- Step four: Write down what the best-case scenarios could be. What is the best that could happen?

Through completing this exercise, you will often realize that the worst-case scenarios aren't really that bad. Plus, you will be more ready for them if they do happen. In fact, often you will see that actions are worth taking that risk to achieve the best-case scenarios. Eventually you will become comfortable with those results and understand how you would overcome them. Follow the four steps of fear setting anytime you are facing a challenge.

"I may wish to be free from torture, but if the time comes for me to endure it, I'll wish to bear it courageously with bravery and honor."– Seneca

Practicing misfortune

In modern times we experience a comfortable quality of life. A warm bed, food in the fridge and a roof over our heads. Whether you consider yourself lucky or not you're probably better off than most people in the world. Certainly, more so than over two thousand years ago. However, being in such comfort we often forget how fortunate our circumstances are. But what if we didn't have such comforts?

Practicing misfortune is an exercise the Stoics used to help them to appreciate the comforts they had. In order to practice misfortune, one goes about giving up some of their comforts for a short period of time. The theory behind it is that we carry anxiety and doubts about losing what we have which holds us back from taking risks to become better. However, if we practice living as if we lost that which we fear losing then it makes us stronger and more comfortable with taking risks towards growth. Furthermore, it makes us more grateful for what we have.

Consider how you could practice misfortune. Maybe you eat the same meal every day for a week. Or you live in a basic apartment for a month. Or you sleep on the floor for a week. Imagine you lost all your money. As a result, you would have to live much more frugally. Try it out and see how it would feel for you. Probably you will realize that it's not all that bad. I once went to live with monks for a few days where I slept on the floor of a wooden hut in the forest. Yet during that time I slept so well. In conclusion of the experience, I realized that if everything went wrong in my life I could come and live there. I was ok with that. In fact, I was happy there free from materialism and attachments.

Seneca himself said that each month we should set aside some days to practice poverty. Have a little food, wear cheap clothes and escape from your comforts. Then ask yourself "Is this what I really dread?". Comfort can make you a slave and keep you trapped from the life you truly want. Prepare yourself and make yourself comfortable with being uncomfortable. Not only will it make you stronger it will also give you more confidence to take those risks towards rewards.

In addition to building more mental toughness it's wise to build a strong body. The ancient Stoics advised that students should practice cold exposure and fasting because they knew that too much comfort is a weakness. Seneca, who was a rich man, practiced fasting and was often underdressed for cold weather. Fasting and cold exposure are great for health. Science has found that they can strengthen immunity and make us more tolerant to pain. In addition, we should also implement a weekly exercise regime.

Work on having the best health you can. Take care of your body. Eat healthy food and do not overindulge. Get into a regular exercise routine. Make sure you get plenty of sleep. Cut out any things which negatively affect your health. To live your best life, it helps to have a healthy body and mind. The better care you take of your health the more life you have to enjoy. You live longer and function better. Lift weights and build strength. Run and improve your cardiovascular system. Eat healthy and clean. These habits will build you a healthy and strong body. A body that can handle a strong mind. A body that can deal with stress and fight for a better life.

Memento Mori

One last thing on negative thinking! Meditate on death to bring clarity to your life. We will all die one day. In fact, during our lifetime, we will die many times. The child dies to become an adult. The single man dies to become a husband and so on. Our existence is fragile. Think about where you were five years ago. How quickly did that time pass? Imagine how quickly the next five years will pass. Life could stop at any moment, and you never know when that moment might be. Accepting death is a life philosophy we should all practice. When we die, we return back to a state of nonexistence.

One day you are going to die. There is no escaping that. Acknowledging this will help you to waste less time on the things that are not important. Indeed, life can be long enough to do what matters. But it is still short enough to waste. Ultimately time cannot be taken back. Allow this to drive the actions you take and let it motivate you to spend your time wisely. Don't think about this as all doom and gloom. But rather as a way to motivate you to be more specific, purposeful and meaningful in the way you live. Remind yourself that time is your most precious commodity.

"It's not that we have a short time to live, but that we waste a lot of it." –Seneca

Ultimately, we cannot be truly alive whilst we are consumed by fears and the ultimate fear, death. The philosophy of Memento Mori which is the Stoic contemplation of death helps one to be fearless in the face of death. The ancient Stoics were well aware of their mortality. Life is short and they realized that death was coming one day. Death is outside of our control and so we should remain indifferent to it. When one becomes sad and overwhelmed by death one must realize that it is their impression or judgment of the event which distresses them. Death doesn't have to be a bad thing. Only when you associate that judgment to it. See life as a temporary thing and allow that to motivate you to excel.

For those of us who have come close to death we can understand how much it makes you prioritize what is important in life. For most we realize what our true values are. Understand that externals such as wealth and reputation cannot be taken with us to the grave. To accept our death helps us to rise above petty troubles. Stoicism calls this magnanimity which is to have a big soul and a vast mind. Magnanimity helps one to rise above everything. When one can accept the certainty of their death then they are on the way to Stoic magnanimity. They are on the way to expanding beyond their troubles. To be free of pain and pleasure.

Every night Seneca reminded himself that he might not awaken to live the next day.   Marcus Aurelius constantly contemplated his own death, imagining himself to be already dead and living on borrowed time. Such contemplation helps one to realize that most worries in life are trivial. Too often we run away from the facts of life. Instead, we need to face them head on. Indeed, it might seem dark and depressing to meditate on your mortality. However, on the contrary it can be utilized as a tool to understand meaning and priority. To make one realize what is important and what is not. To make us use our time on earth wisely and to not waste it. This brings us closer to living the life we want to live. Don't be the one who finds out they have months to live and then start a bucket list. Live now.

"Those whom you love and those whom you despise will both be made equal in the same ashes" — Seneca, Moral Letters

PRINCIPLES FOR INNER PEACE & HAPPINESS

Happiness is what makes us uniquely human. Other animals don't experience these kinds of emotions. The definition of happiness is to be cheerful and to have enjoyable experiences. Most people associate it with external factors which are largely out of our control. For example, being healthy, rich or having a stable family. Stoicism teaches us that if you live in the right way then happiness will result. We have covered this before, which is to live in alignment with nature. We are therefore responsible for our own happiness. Any external thing that we might think brings us happiness is really something indifferent. Whether that is wealth, health, social status, material possessions and so on.

The ancient Stoics realized that happiness depends on your own efforts and qualities. Virtue and the qualities of character are critical to this. Developing our virtue and character, wisdom, courage, justice and self-control depends on us. Essentially if you live according to the virtues, you will be happy. According to Stoicism we can be happy without possession of externals because they do not make a difference between being happy or sad. Indeed, it is possible to have a good life without them. As long as you exercise the virtues. When we experience negative emotions, it is usually based on a false judgment that some external thing is good or bad. When we lose something, we think has value it causes us sadness. Or when we associate happiness with something fleeting. Good emotions are more consistent and longer lasting. When we can learn to accept our fate and non-permanent view of life we can detach from those externals and live in alignment with nature.

Almost two thousand years ago Stoic philosophers set out on their journeys to find inner peace and happiness. They created practices and rituals to cultivate inner peace and happiness. To this day all of us want peace of mind. For some of us it is easier said than done. These days life is moving so fast. We are in a rush from the moment we wake up. Social media and entertainment keep us distracted in those moments of boredom and tiredness. But in those moments, we need to search for stillness. Take time for your mind to unwind and to do nothing. If you're not allowing your mind to do that then you will probably struggle to sleep at night. In bed your mind races and processes the day's events. Don't let that happen. Instead during the day let your mind unwind naturally. Take time out for short walks, journaling or just chilling out.

Gratitude

Gratitude is the foundation of a happier and stronger mind. Stoicism teaches us that   wanting less will increase gratitude whilst wanting more will reduce it. In psychology this is known as hedonic adaptation. When we are grateful, we transition from those feelings of lack or not having what we want. Essentially it breaks the cycle of wanting and needing. Furthermore, it can break you free from jealousy and envy. When one is grateful for what they have they desire less and as a result they feel happier with what they have now. The ancient Stoics were focused on reducing the desire of wanting more and in turn cultivating more gratitude. When we let go of pursuing or wanting more and fearing what we may lose it frees us to be in the present moment. Epictetus called gratitude 'eucharistos' which is the art of seeing the truth of what is happening in each moment.

Imagine the farmer in a poor rural village versus the high-powered corporate executive. Who do you think is happier? Probably the farmer because he is grateful for having what he has, a family around him and a simple life. Whilst the executive is always chasing desire. Yes, it is good to have goals to go for. But more stuff won't necessarily make you happier. Appreciation of it will make you happy and gratitude is the key to that. Realize how lucky you are to be living in this world. The very fact that you're here and living is a miracle in itself. Stoicism teaches us to be aware of our mortality in order to be grateful for the shortness of life. Don't let the small stuff get you down. Meditate on the big picture and on the uniqueness of you being here. Be present to the moment. Focus on the here and now. Forget about your worries or regrets. Most of the time we worry about things that never even end up happening.

"When you arise in the morning, think of what a precious privilege it is to be alive."

– Marcus Aurelius

Accept your fate and be grateful for literally everything, including the bad stuff. Be grateful for everything that happens to you because it is all part of the universe's grand scheme. Furthermore, it is not just about being personally grateful but for the whole of our universe. We should also seek and celebrate the advancement of our friends as much as we do for ourselves. This is living in alignment with nature. True it's not easy to be grateful for those setbacks, bad experiences and so on. But it is all possible. For example, maybe that failed relationship led you to the love of your life. Or maybe losing your job led to you starting a business. Often, we are just one step away from our destiny. See every perceived set back as a step closer. Focus on the positive things in your life. Even though some things might not work out your way, it's all about perspective. Realize that in the big picture you're still here and living. Realize that every bad situation often has a silver lining. All that happens to you is for the reason to shape who you are and bring you to where you need to be. Understanding this will help you to become more grateful.

Practicing gratitude

Practicing gratitude is important because it doesn't come by itself. It needs to be cultivated. All of us are born on different points of happiness. Gratitude has been proven many times to raise that. Make an intentional choice to be grateful and happy for everything. The ancient Stoics believed in appreciating what we have in life and never taking anything for granted and to never complain. Complaining only keeps you in an ungrateful state which hurts you. Again, it is useless because it's focused on the past which cannot be changed. Learn from the past. Don't live there. Put your energy into having a better present and future. Quit complaining because it archives nothing. Accept that you cannot change the world or the people in it.

"He is wise who doesn't grieve for the things he doesn't have but rejoices for the things he does have." –Epictetus

Journaling

According to the Harvard Business School journaling is a proven way to increase gratitude, performance, manage stress and gain clearer thinking. Try keeping a gratitude journal where you can write about all the things, you're grateful for. This practice will help you to cultivate more gratitude in your life. Every morning I like to write down at least ten things I am grateful for. They can be anything, from the small to the big things. For example, the air I breathe or for having my family. I like to write them all down. Everyday it's different. Just ask yourself what you're grateful for today and let your pen flow. Think about how they make you feel. Practice this during the day in your mind also. In fact, anytime you feel down it can be a powerful antidote.

Marcus Aurelius the great Stoic and Roman emperor wrote one of the most famous journals in history, Meditations. It was his private journal which after his death became public knowledge. Those minutes he spent alone each day with his journal helped to turn him into one of the greatest men to ever live in the world. The miracle of his journal surviving almost two thousand years proves its value. Reflecting on one's thoughts onto paper was a common practice back then. Each person has their own way of journaling. The purpose of Stoic journaling is not necessarily about recording your own history. You can also use it to reflect on your life or to work things out. Or maybe just to clear your head and to solve the mental issues you have going on. For Marcus Aurelius the purpose of journaling was to remind himself of how to live a virtuous life.

Stoicism says that we have control over our inner world. Through introspection, self-awareness and gratitude we can become our best self. Reflect on your life. Acknowledge your negative and positive sides. Work on them. Continue to grow and develop inner strength with journaling. Make the time for it. Sacrifice some of your texting and social media time. Wake up in the morning and use your journal to write about whatever is on your mind at that time. Also, throughout the day you will be likely to have some ideas or important things come up. Make a note of them. This could be on your phone note pad to make it easier to record. The more you do this the more capacity your brain has to be inventive. Sometimes the best ideas come completely out of the blue. Make sure you take note of them. Or at the end of the day take some time to reflect on it. What went well? What didn't go well? How could you have made it better? Let it flow out onto the paper. Don't hold back. Consider it like a kind of private therapy. The path to greatness comes from self-reflection and awareness.

Allow yourself to write whatever you feel. There are no rules so don't censor yourself. Use it to consult with yourself, make better decisions and to gain clarity of mind. Free your mind to live life in the present moment. Allow the darkest secrets, fears, anxieties, dreams and whatever to come out. Start with just writing in the morning for five minutes or so. Maybe you could answer a few prompts such as what you're grateful for or what's currently a challenge for you. It doesn't need to be outstanding grammar and perfect writing. Just start writing and let it flow. Stream of conscious journaling is one of the most useful ways to relieve stress and become happier. Let your thoughts flow onto the paper.

Think of some of the most important questions you ask yourself. Perhaps those are questions such as. Why do I want to be rich? How can I become rich? What kind of relationship do I want? Who brings out the best in me? How can I become a better person? What am I grateful for? And so on. Have them written in your journal as writing triggers. You could do these in the morning, evening or when it is suitable. Write out what your goals are. Those can be your vision, long term and in the short term. Write them out in detail. Brainstorm how to get there. What you need. Take inventory and map it out. Bring it all into your awareness.

CONCLUSION

Stoicism is about conquering yourself and it gives us a blueprint by which we can live our best lives. Think of it like a life code which gives you answers to questions and ways of how to conduct yourself. When we embrace it, we can be free from so much of the mental activity that tires us out. Some might think this a restrictive way of living but for the ancient Stoics they believed it releases us from anxiety and uncertainty. In turn this brings us peace and a path to follow. Now let us conclude this book by going over what we have learned on our journey.

We began this book by talking about the problems of modern society. Now more than ever it has become fragmented and disconnected. We are lost and seeking answers to why our life doesn't match the ideal portrayed in the media. False illusions convince us that we need more things to be happy. Maybe, more wealth, materialism and love are the answers. Yet we end up in lonely pursuits disconnected from our true nature. Looking for answers we get lost in all the endless stream of gurus and self-help or we act selfishly in the pursuit of our solo endeavors. Ancient Stoics two thousand years ago also realized that happiness doesn't come from the material possessions around us. They understood that events are not inherently good or bad. Our mind is what decides upon that. Status symbols such as wealth and fame are indeed preferred to their opposite, but they are not essential to living a good life. As long as one has the right frame of mind then they can live well regardless of most situations.

Stoicism was developed as a way to help people live their best lives. Yet many people have avoided it because they think that they will need to turn off their emotions or that they will not have any more pleasures anymore. Well that as we have seen in this book it is just not the truth. What we have discovered is that you don't need to follow any religious practices, and neither will you need to throw away all your possessions or live isolated from society. However, living the way of a Stoicism is going to require a personal reinvention. In doing so the promise of this life is tranquility, to deal with negative emotions more effectively and in turn have a stronger character who is living their best life.

At the beginning of this book, we explored the origins of Stoicism. This is important to understand because it paints a full picture of where it came from and who the famous philosophers from ancient history were. We can understand their minds and what was going on in their lives at that time it was created. Indeed, they also suffered many of the anxieties and problems that we now face. Again, that's why Stoicism is such a timeless philosophy.

Moving on we took a look at the foundations of Stoicism. The universe guides and connects all of us together. Think of it as being God in everything. When one considers themself in isolation from the universe then they're going to suffer in misery. When one realizes that one is part of the universe, they can start to make decisions that live in alignment with nature and that is a virtuous life. Goodness comes from understanding our place in the universe and collaborating with it for all of our benefit. This is the foundation of Stoicism which is living virtuously. Happiness is a by-product of this way of living.

To further explain the foundations of Stoicism we took a look at the happiness triangle consisting of Eudaimonia at the center which is the goal of life. Essentially it means to flourish. Connected to it on the triangle are to "Live with Arete" which is to become your best self. That requires developing your character to the highest levels and closing the gap between who you are now and who your best self is. The other points on that triangle are to take responsibility for everything in your life and to be aware of what you control.

In the next chapter we explored virtue which is the true pathway to happiness. To live virtuously we need to be aware of the four cardinal virtues which are wisdom, temperance, justice and moderation. At the opposite end is vice which brings negativity whilst in the middle are gray indifferents which doesn't necessarily contribute to happiness. Rather they are just preferred or not preferred. When we misjudge them is when we evaluate something as being more than what is necessary for happiness. Regardless of our background one can live virtuously and that will be its own reward. If you struggle with living virtuously, ask yourself questions in the situation you are facing. Pass them through the four cardinals to determine whether it's worthwhile for you to take action or to avoid that situation.

Moving on we explored the dichotomy of control which is one

of the most popular teachings of Stoicism. In summary life can be divided into what we control and what we don't control. Realize that there is very little you control and when you try to control what you cannot, you will become emotionally disturbed by it. Ultimately what you really do control is your internal world. Focus on this and leave the rest in God's hands. Stoicism calls this Amor Fati, which is the love of our fate. We must love whatever comes to us because it's not in our power. Focus on what you control, which is your internal world, let go of the rest and accept your fate.

In the next chapter we explored desires. Since the beginning of time desires have led us astray. All too often they have led to unhealthy passions, compulsions and obsessions. According to Stoicism a human consumed by desire is akin to a human acting as an animal. Realize that there are so many temptations and desires coming at us. Therefore, we have to take responsibility for not being led astray. Often, we need to delay gratification and, in this chapter, we explored how to do that effectively. We looked at keyways for dealing with temptations that can lead us astray. Stoicism suggests the concept of Apatheia which is the mind-state free from emotional disturbance. Again, this isn't about depriving yourself. Instead, it guides one to divide passions into unhealthy and healthy. A well-trained Stoic understands the difference. Seneca said we should enjoy pleasures that come to us, to act reasonably with them and to not overindulge. Of course, everything in moderation is fine. But we must also remain indifferent to them because one day we will lose them.

Moving forward we explored emotions. Again, I'm highlighting here that Stoicism is not the suppression of emotions. Mastery of emotions is the goal here and to not be carried away by them. In this chapter we explored how to gain mastery of your emotions and their inner workings. We took a look at the three stages of emotions which are stimulus, perception and response. Understanding these three stages identifies the gap between stimulus to perception and response. We're all affected by stimulus, whoever we are. Ultimately that's up to nature and you can't change that. However, we have the ability of applying reason to look at perceptions objectively and then to determine the right course of response which aligns with nature.

Additionally in exploring emotions we have dived deep into the toxic emotions namely anger, stress, jealousy and envy. We took a deep dive into those emotions to understand what they are and how to deal with them effectively. Stoicism works very well here because those emotions were studied thoroughly by ancient stoics. Again, it's a timeless philosophy which has worked on humans for thousands of years. In reality these negative emotions are based on incorrect judgements which lead us to unpleasant experiences and actions. As Seneca said they are a temporary madness and should be avoided at all costs because all too often they lead us to bad endings.

In the later chapters we took a look at the power of negative thinking, positivity and happiness. I understand that many of you are going to be put off about thinking negatively. However, you must realize that negative emotions often can bring you improvement as we rise from those places of darkness and struggle. Acknowledge them instead of glossing over them. Then we can draw strength from them. The ancient Stoics were well aware of this, and they had some specific practices or negative thinking exercises which were outlined in this chapter.

Premeditatio Malorum is to negatively visualize all the wrong things that could happen to us. Use this exercise for upcoming situations that you might have anxiety about. Determine all the things that could go wrong and how you would deal with them. Furthermore, envision all the best things that could happen. The practice will reveal that it's not so bad which will probably motivate you to go ahead and take action.

Next, we explored how the Stoics practice misfortune. Essentially this is to put ourselves in uncomfortable situations for a short period of time. Become comfortable with the uncomfortable and it will make you stronger when faced with adversity. Death is a guarantee of life. Sorry to be so negative but there is no escaping that fact. Memento Mori is the old famous Stoic concept of meditating on your death. Accepting that one day you will day will help you to appreciate and make the most of your life. Furthermore, accept the mortality of your friends and family. Let that motivate you to make the most of your time with them. Make peace with accepting your mortality. I know that sounds very dark and dreadful but it's in fact a great way to look at the shortness of life. Allow that to motivate you and to not waste time.

In the final chapter we explored positivity and happiness which of course is what we all want. Now that all depends on your efforts and living virtuously. When you live according to nature it is a virtuous way of living which will in turn make you happy. We explored here that gratitude is the foundation of a happy and strong mind. We need to be grateful for what we have. When we want less it will increase our gratitude. Whilst wanting more makes us needy and unhappy. Transition from those feelings of want or not having.

Stoicism teaches us to be grateful for literally everything including the bad experiences because in the bigger picture we are still living. Right now, we don't know if those bad experiences are really good or not. Maybe in the long run they will lead us towards something better. Therefore, we need to cultivate more gratitude. Journaling is a great way of bringing into your awareness of what you are already grateful for. Marcus Aurelius wrote one of the most famous journals. In it he explored his gratitude and reflected on his life. Self-reflection is the key to improving oneself.

Marcus Aurelius was the emperor of Rome. He likely had access to unlimited luxury. But he did not obsess over luxury. He was a wise man who found beauty in simplicity. Noting that simple things are beautiful in their own unique way. Take a look at the sky for example and be humbled by it. Walk out in nature and take it all in. Stoicism teaches us that the universe is a vast and unexplained place. We are humans who need to appreciate our place in it. Remember that the foundation of Stoicism is the universe that we are all connected through. Living in alignment with nature is all about understanding our place in the universe. We have to realize that we're all connected together like a large entity. Our life should encompass the greater good of humanity because that is a virtuous way of living. Ultimately this requires an assent to providence. Essentially that is to be guided by God.

Inside of us we have a personal God and when we let our characters turn bad, giving into the devil inside then negative events occur. That is the real demon of life. Indeed, it is often easier said than done. When those external distractions and desires come up it can be at times difficult to say no. Take care of your fellow humans to lift them up and to do good things for them. Yes, this seems like a lot of responsibility but when you act that way it's going to be virtuous. Happiness will be a byproduct of it. Help people to become better including becoming a better person yourself because it will lift up our society.

Thousands of years ago the Stoics figured a way of living with less suffering and more enjoyment. At its core Stoicism is a philosophy for happiness. Living a meaningful and happy life is the deepest desire of humans. We want to feel important and connected in the world. We want to be proud of the life we are living. Ultimately, we want to live our best life. We want to share that life with the people we love. Living your best life requires being your best self. Life's a journey of ups and downs. We all know this. Stoicism will help you to ride through it all. It will help you to be capable of expiring both pleasure and pain without them causing ruin.

Seneca reminds us through his letters that alongside the pursuit of virtue we should strive for something meaningful in life. Our focus should be on cultivating a mind of excellence. This requires us to pay attention to the judgments we make and to develop positive character traits such as wisdom, courage, moderation and justice. These virtues will help us to become better people and act true to live in alignment with nature. The only true good is to have a virtuous character and a rational mind. This as the Stoics would say is the requirement of living a good life.

I wish you all the best on your journey to living The Way of The Stoic. Please revisit this book again and again to refresh the philosophy of Stoicism in your mind. Now if you would please kindly take the time to leave a review of this book where you purchased it.

Thank you and good luck my friend.

WAY OF THE SPARTAN

LIFE LESSONS TO STRENGTHEN YOUR CHARACTER, BUILD MENTAL TOUGHNESS, MINDSET, SELF-DISCIPLINE & A HEALTHY BODY

THOMAS SWAIN

INTRODUCTION

Modern society is weak. We live in a permanent comfort zone. Wrapped up in cotton wool. Every day you can easily just stay at home. Order food delivery from your phone to your door. Order furniture delivery right to your door. Heck you can even mail order a bride! Have a digital relationship. In fact, you never have to set foot outside your house again. You could just stay in bed all day watching reruns on Netflix. But does it make you happy?

It seems like nowadays people are ok with living a below average life. Wake up, work at a boring job, come home watch the same stuff on TV and eat cheap low-quality food.

Then when life throws obstacles at us, we aren't dealing with them properly. We pacify our behaviors through escape. Escaping to drugs, vices and distractions. However, those all end up feeding a beast and growing it. In the end it simply makes things worse.

Problem is we don't have any initiation. We were just taught at school how to be a good worker. Get a nine to five job, get married, settle down and that's as high as ambition goes for most people. We were never taught about how to set and go after goals. We were never taught about how to deal with the frustration, disappointment and adversity of life. We are lacking ambition and there is so much dissatisfaction with life. Plus, we are now overwhelmed and lack the structure to deal with it. Why do we put up with that?

Sorry to paint such a negative picture, but it's the truth. Don't hide it. Acknowledge and own the fact because it can be used to your advantage. The truth is that we all want something better for our lives. But nothing worthwhile comes easily. Courage and a strong mindset are required. To live your best life, you're going to have to step outside of your comfort zone. You have to dare to be great. The Spartan way shows you how.

The Spartans were strong warriors and there is a lot to learn from them. Based in ancient Greece they were famous for their mental and physical toughness. Incidentally they have gone down in history as some of the most mentally tough people ever. Their legacy was created at the battle of Thermopylae, which is depicted in the modern movie, 300. The epic battle saw a small army of 300 Spartan soldiers fight to the death against a huge Persian army. It went down in history as one of the true stands against a huge enemy. A legacy that was possible due to the Spartan training and ways of living.

They might have been around thousands of years ago, but their legacy has lasted till this day. There's a lot to learn from them that's for sure. Now you're not likely to be going into battle these days. No one is going to pillage your home and decapitate you. However, if you're reading this I know you probably want more from life. Learning from the Spartan way of life will help you to get to what you want. In this book you'll learn how they became mentally tough and the values they lived by. The way of The Spartan.

Most things of value require effort, patience and hard work. You will learn all of that here. Spartan life principles and lessons will allow you to deal with life challenges as they come and steamroll over them. Or slay them like a Spartan! Furthermore, their philosophy can be applied to modern life to make sure you are living your best life. That will help you to avoid the trappings of life that make people weak. In addition, they were also physical specimens. Muscular and powerful with bodies built for war that were capable of incredible accomplishments. You can feel just like them, you can feel like a warrior, a powerful warrior. Plus, it won't require any fancy gym technology or fad diets. It's pure, simple and powerful knowledge from the legendary warriors.

Whether you're an executive seeking to climb the ladder or a student pushing towards better grades. You could even be a parent looking to teach good values to their children. This book shows you how and much more. Live your legacy and follow the Spartan Way.

To begin we are going to explore their history to understand how they became so great, strong and powerful. Let's begin our journey now.

SPARTAN HISTORY

The city of Sparta was a strong military state located within ancient Greece. It grew to become a city rivalling the capital of Athens and peaked in power around 404 BC. Sparta became famous and feared for its numerous triumphs in battles. In its prime the city had no walls. Instead preferring to defend it with men. Two kings ruled at a time to ensure that when one king went out on a military campaign another would stay to rule the society. Focus was all in on military power. The society of Sparta was divided into conquered people who did not have citizenship and the Spartans. The conquered population included a group called the Helots who were responsible for agricultural and daily tasks to support the Spartans. The Spartans priority was military training in preparation for battle.

Sparta had a warrior cult, military dominance and independent women. Discipline and loyalty to the state were second to none for the Spartans. Incidentally in modern times the word "Spartan" has come to describe discipline and mental toughness. Shortly after birth males were evaluated. According to the historian Plutarch, only healthy Spartans survived. Unfortunately, those who were unhealthy were left to die at the foot of a mountain because the goal was to produce healthy babies who would then become strong soldiers. Females were to be with their mothers. Whilst the strong male children at the age of just seven years old left their families and began training for the army.

The Spartans became strong and powerful due to their harsh and extreme training methods which would turn boys into soldiers. Education and training were very strict. If they were caught doing anything wrong, they were severely punished. Any signs of cowardice were seen as a crime. As a part of their tough training, they were flogged at the sanctuary of Artemis Orthia to show their toughness and endurance. The training aimed to install virtues of strength, endurance and solidarity.

To make them even tougher Spartan boys were usually barefoot and rarely bathed or used ointments. Their skin became tough, hard and dry. For their clothing they were given a single cloak for the whole year. This made them tougher and able to endure cold or heat at the extremes. Plants were torn from the riverbanks with their bare hands to make their beds. A meager and natural diet kept them lean whilst it also made them resourceful and rigorous. This all added to their regime of building strong minds and bodies which were regularly inspected. Those who were not up to par would be flogged.

Physical fitness was a focus of training, and the soldiers were encouraged to fight each other. Fear was regularly faced. Spartan physical training was designed to make boys strong and fit. The training primarily focused on gymnastics, singing and dancing. In addition to physical fitness the Spartan troops relentlessly drilled tactics until perfection. Tactical maneuver mastery gave them a distinct advantage in battles. Mindsets of toughness and wisdom cultivated from their training gave them further advantages.

Training was divided into different age groups. Boys from the age of seven to seventeen were taught writing, reading, singing and dancing. Older boys from eighteen to nineteen were trained for the army. Youths from twenty to twenty-nine years old then went onto the toughest military training for the army. Men then had to remain in military barracks until the age of thirty. Then those adults above thirty years old would become citizens and were expected to marry. Spartans continued training throughout their adulthood right up until the age of sixty. Then they could retire as an elder. If they lived that long.

To be frank their training was absolutely brutal. After such rigorous training a war would seem like a nice holiday to them! Fighting and training was so important to them that they outsourced everything else. Experts were hired to do everything else from their taxes to sharpening their weapons and anything else other than training or fighting. This allowed them to focus on what was most important to them. Willpower would therefore not be depleted and instead conserved for the battles that lay ahead. This gave the Spartans an extra advantage over their enemies. That's why they were so feared.

The Battle of Thermopylae

Otherwise known as the 300, The Battle of Thermopylae in 480 BC was one of the most famous battles of the Spartans. In this battle the Spartan king Leonidas led a small army into a battle against a gigantic Persian army that has gone down in history as one of the most courageous last stands. Let's go back in time and look at how it unfolded.

Leonidas was a king of Sparta until his death at the Battle of Thermopylae. As king he was both a military and political leader. Just like all male Spartans, he was trained since childhood in preparation to become a strong warrior. His enemy Xerxes the ruler of a vast Persian empire invaded Greece in 480 BC. Xeres was feared by many and was known as a "God King". A huge army of soldiers was assembled from all regions of his vast empire and rampaged through ancient Greece without opposition. City after city bowed to them. However, upon reaching the pass of Thermopylae, Xerxes' army hit an obstacle. It was there that he encountered The Spartan army waiting. Led by the Spartan king Leonidas the ensuing battle went down in history as an epic.

"The world will know that free men stood against a tyrant, that few stood against many, and before this battle was over, even a god-king can bleed." - 300

Thermopylae is a mountainous area in southern Greece. Due to such terrain the invading Persians had to travel along the coast and go through a narrow pass. This is where the Spartans tactically waited for them in anticipation. The narrow pass gave them an advantage since the large Persian army could only cross a certain number of troops through there at a time. The pass was only wide enough to allow a few hundred at a time therefore making it impossible to bring their full forces through at once.

Herodotus says that the Persians who were sure of an easy victory first sent a messenger to ask the Spartans to surrender. Lay down their arms and retreat peacefully they asked. King Leonidas has become legendary for saying: "Come and take them." Frustrated at the Spartan's defiance after five days the Persians attacked. Into the narrow pass they funneled through and were met by a tactical formation of Spartan soldiers. Set into the narrow pass, the Spartans were devastatingly effective. The first wave of attacks was deadly, but they were easily fought off by the Spartans. Then followed a second attack of some of the Persians' finest warriors, called the Immortals. Yet Xerxes watched his best soldiers perish.

Over the next few days, the battle raged on. The Persians lost many soldiers whilst The Spartans sustained just a few losses. However, it was a betrayal that set in motion their downfall. Seeking reward from the Persian God king, a local shepherd offered to show a hidden pathway which the Persians could use to bypass the Spartans and then launch a surprise attack. Xerxes dispatched a force of men who marched through the night.

King Leonidas, faced with certain defeat, ordered most of his men to leave. Only a small army remained to hold off the Persians for as long as possible. Those remaining men were the famous 300 Spartans. In the mid-morning Xerxes made his final attack and the Persians closed in. Outnumbered and surrounded The Spartans fought to the death displaying great strength and a heroic fight until the death. Ultimately the sheer force of numbers of Persians overwhelmed the smaller Spartan army. King Leonidas was slain as the remaining Spartans made their last stand.

Ultimately the Spartans perished against the mighty Persian army, but the battle lives on because of the bravery, sacrifice and toughness of the Spartans. In the face of overwhelming challenge and fear they fought on. Even with an outnumbered force they made a significant toll on the enemy. It was their tactical use of military advantages and toughness that helped them when they were far outnumbered.

Even though the battle was a loss for the Spartans it went down in history as a victory over tyranny. A victory of courage over fear. Forever they went down in history as legendary warriors. A legacy cemented. Thanks to the epic battle of Thermopylae where a small army of Spartan soldiers fought to the death against a much larger Persian army, the legacy of Sparta lives on. To this day the word "Spartan" brings up associations of strength and courage. It's time we learn from their legend.

SPARTAN MENTAL TOUGHNESS

With just 300 Spartan warriors, the great king Leonidas held back the mighty Persian army. This unbreakable courage, strength and willpower was a manifestation of Spartan values. To the outsider The Spartans probably seemed like some talented warriors. Were they even human? They seem to be almost mythical. Indeed, they were human and indeed they came from harsh times. However seemingly mythical talents were not all of who they were. It was dedication and mental toughness that carved them into warriors. Warriors with the mental toughness to do what needed to get done.

Imagine being mentally tough like the Spartan Warriors. They were the epitome of perseverance despite insurmountable obstacles. Since then, few have shown such resilience. This is why their legacy lasts till this day. Modern society has fallen far from them. We are infected with worriers, wimps and whiners. Of course, we no longer live in the days where our heads could be decapitated by an axe wielding enemy. But there are still wars to fight. Not wars against armies but wars against our demons and distractions. Every day you will have to go to war against the demons inside of your head telling you to stop or take a rest. It's a new type of war. Having physical and mental toughness is a distinct advantage to winning those wars. Whether they are in the gym at home or at the office.

So how can you be mentally tough like a Spartan? Well, you might think you're weak or unworthy right now but the best part is that mental toughness can be learned and increased. Various mental conditioning processes exist that can turn the mentally weak into the strong. One of the most effective principles to build mental toughness is to condition yourself to embrace discomfort on a frequent basis. The process of pushing boundaries will help you to adapt and in turn grow stronger. These challenges can be things such as taking the stairs instead of the elevator. Waiting a little bit longer to eat. Spending more time doing something productive and so on. Essentially, it's about breaking out of your comfort zone.

Spartans despised the comfort zone and they hated weakness.

Following on are some specific ways to build mental toughness. Stick with these and try them for at least a month. Give your brain time to adapt and grow.

Optimism & Persistence

Tough times make strong men. Too much comfort makes a person weak. Tough times define us and show us what we are made of. We should be grateful for them. We should be optimists who persist through the challenges towards their goals. Optimists clearly know what they want to accomplish and when obstacles come along as they always will, they persist. That's because they believe in themselves and that gives them the confidence to overcome any obstacles that might come their way. Have an optimistic attitude towards life. Persist when things get tough. Look for the lessons in those negative experiences. Stay focused on what you want and focus on how to get there. Optimism and persistence are the way towards your dreams.

Compete only with yourself

Everyone is on their own journey. Each person has their own unique advantages along the way. We all come from different backgrounds and circumstances. That's why it's pointless to compare yourself with others. Doing so will only make you feel worse. After all, you can always find someone better off than you. But if you compare who you are today to who you were before then you can gain confidence from that knowledge. Because if you're on your path towards a goal then naturally you will be constantly improving. The Spartans never thought about how good their enemy may be. No, instead they focused on their power and improving it.

Enjoy the moment

This book talks a lot about goals. But most important is the journey. Enjoy each moment. Failure to do so could mean wasted time. Imagine if the Spartans were focused only on the next event. They would have been slain. We would have never known about them. Enjoy what you do and savor each moment. Unplug. Our modern world is switched on and plugged in twenty-four hours a day seven days a week. But it's not natural for humans to be constantly engaged in concentration. Yet this is what's happening nowadays. Our devices keep us engaged all the time. Take the time to unplug and let your brain relax and strategize. Imagine the great king Leonidas walking up in the mountains to reflect and recharge. Meditation is another way of being more in the present moment. Take ten to twenty minutes a day out. Be with yourself and your breathing. I recommend the works of Eckhart Tolle for more on the present moment.

Also take time to reflect. In this world of chaos, it can be easy to become overwhelmed. When you feel that way it's time for you to break away and reflect. Sit in silence. Tune out the noise. Give yourself some space to let go. The mind needs time to unwind and process the day's events. Remember King Leonidas who walked in the mountains. Escape out into nature. Go for a walk and disconnect from the world. Practice doing this every day and you will build strong mental powers.

Patience

Patience is a virtue of life. That means it's a blessing to have and it's something we must cultivate. Success won't happen overnight. We often need to wait a bit longer than necessary. Be the one who can wait a bit longer and you're going to get that bit further than the others who give up too early. Practice being patient. Find situations that typically make you impatient. Go into them fully and embrace it. You don't need to rush anything. Rome wasn't built in a day and neither was Spartan power built overnight. It took them many years to become warriors. And their journey never stopped.

Learn from failure

Too many people perceive failure as being the end. They run away. Failure for most means it's time for them to give up and hide away from their shame. But those who are mentally tough see failures as something to learn from. Something to improve upon. A step closer to their destiny. That's why the Spartans trained every day. In doing so they could discover their weaknesses through failure and seek to improve upon them. Often there is something great that comes from failure. You just have to look for the lesson and be open to learning from it.

Personally, when faced with what seems like a failure I like to think of the story "Three feet from gold" by Napoleon Hill. In this story a man hears of a hidden gold mine. Treasure beyond imagination. He hires a time and spends the next few years drilling holes with expensive mining equipment. Yet too soon he finds nothing and gives up. Another man hears about this new opportunity. He takes up the mining contract and discovers the previous miner was just three feet from gold. Now he is the one who becomes wealthy beyond his wildest dreams. When you hit those obstacles and failures don't think of them as failures. Think of them as being closer to your goals. Believe in you. You're now just three feet from gold.

Visualize

The great Spartan king Leonidas visualized his plan of trapping the giant Persian army in the narrow path of Thermopylae. Mentally he envisioned the success of his warriors. Adopt the same mentality. When you have an event of importance coming up or a goal you want to achieve. Visualize it. See the details and put yourself in the moment. When that moment comes you will be more ready for it.

"Every time I feel tired while exercising and training, I close my eyes to see that picture, to see that list with my name. This usually motivates me to work again." - Michael Jordan (Basketball)

Finish

Whatever you set out to do, go all in. If you plan to workout at the gym for sixty minutes of a program, then go all in on it. Finish it. If you have an assignment due, finish it. Leave no ends open and take no prisoners. Slay your tasks like a Spartan warrior slaying their enemies. You will gain confidence in finishing what you started. That will build momentum and spiral upwards to more success.

Start the day right

Every day you probably are faced with many commitments to fulfill. But the day needs to start with you. Make the time for yourself to prepare for the day ahead. Maybe that's taking time for you to meditate, stretch, read a book and so on. Put yourself first and you will be stronger for the day ahead. Plus, you will have more time to spend with others fully in the moment later on. Wake up early and it will give you the edge over the competition. Plus, early risers tend to be healthier since they are aligned with the cycles of the Earth. Imagine the Spartans rising in the early morning before their enemies and conquering them whilst they sleep. Establish a sleep cycle that gets you up in the mornings. Even if it means going to bed earlier. Get quality sleep, in a dark and cool room for six to ten hours. When your alarm goes off in the morning, get out of bed and start moving. Never be a sloth who wastes the day in bed or the one who snoozes. Movement will wake up your joints and body. Step outside into the light and let it fill your senses. Get the blood flowing and the day going. Seize the day.

Love

"Live with an open heart even if it hurts" - David Deida

This is a great quote, and it relates well with the Spartans. They loved their wives, families and comrades with an open heart. Yet they were aware of their mortality and that life could be taken away at any moment. In such a dangerous world it would have been easier for them to stay alone and never risk the agony of heartbreak or loss. But they also would have never felt the great depth of love. The love of their comrades, families and wives. Love your family and friends with all your heart. Be open to being hurt but be ok with it. Love is worth it.

Face your fears

Step outside of your comfort zone. The next time someone asks you to do something outside of your comfort zone go for it. What do you really want? Are you willing to go for it? Comfortable lives are nice, but they will keep you from progressing. It's too easy to get complacent in this life. To be happy with the baseline. To be comfortable in your sorrows. But you should strive for more. That often means facing your fears and stepping outside of your comfort zone. The Spartans built better bodies and minds by pushing their limits outside of their comfort zones. They faced giant armies and confronted fear.

We all know about goal setting. But how about a fear setting? Spartans knew what their fears were. That made them more manageable. Try the same. Get some paper and a pen. Define what your fears are. Make a list of all the things that you're hesitant about doing. Next to them list all the worst things that could possibly happen. For example, travelling to a new country. Your fear could be that you will get home sick. Or maybe you have an exam coming. Your fear could be failing. Now make a list of all the things you could do to minimize the chances of these bad things happening. In our examples maybe it's setting up calls whilst you're away from preparing for the exams. Or having a great travel insurance plan in place.

Physical exercise

The Spartans began physical training from an early age. Children had to learn how to survive in the wild. Their training combined resistance, discomfort and endurance. Follow their example. Lift heavy weights. Do this at least three times a week. It will help you to build a powerful physique and push past the mental barriers required to lift heavy weights. You will face adversity but go ahead and conquer it. Make the squat, the bench press and the deadlift the lifts to master. Keep trying to build up your strength. Dedicate yourself to physical training. Become stronger, leaner, faster, better. Every day the Spartans trained hard. If you struggle for time, then do short and intense workouts. Get it done. Discover more about their workouts and diet in the later chapter on Spartan bodies.

Cold showers

Earlier I mentioned how introducing discomfort into your daily routine is a great way to build strength. Cold showers are one of the best ways to create such discomfort and build strength. Naturally you won't want to get into the cold water. But every time you do so you will build more strength. The act of forcing yourself to withstand freezing cold water is both refreshing and builds resilience. Let it spill over your whole body. Calm your breathing as it does. If you struggle at first, make it warm and gradually lower the temperature. That small act of daily courage will spill over into your overall strength and mental toughness.

Fasting

Spartan warriors going out to battle would not always have available food. First and foremost, they had military objectives to fulfill. Fasting made them leaner and tougher.

Mental and physical strengths both benefit from fasting. First it makes you mentally tough and then your body lean. Implement fasting into your day. Try intermittent fasting which involves fasting for sixteen to eighteen hours each day. You can even try fasting for a day or more. Eat a simple diet and never overeat. As a side benefit to being leaner you'll also discover willpower and strength from it.

Learn

It's not all about big muscles and strong bodies. Those will decline with age. Spartans also worked on cultivating intelligence. As elders they advised the kings and army generals. Never stop learning. There is so much to learn. Learn about life, languages, business, relationships and more. Reading is an ancient and powerful method of learning. To this day it's probably one of the most effective ways to learn. It also teaches your mind how to focus for longer. Turn off the distractions and take time to read a good book. Make sure these books are useful and positive to your journey. In addition, you can try some classic games such as chess or doing jigsaws which are all great for brain training and passing the time. Furthermore, find mentors and mastermind groups to build your knowledge and improve yourself.

SPARTAN WILLPOWER

Spartans were famous for their will power. Will power that made it possible to be trained and ready in a harsh world where the enemy could attack at any time. Understandably we don't live in such a world anymore. But the truth is still the same, if you want to achieve something worthwhile then you're going to require will power. With more will power you can focus on eating the right things, avoiding bad situations, exercising regularly, avoiding procrastination, achieving noble goals and much more. For most people a lack of willpower is their most significant barrier to becoming who they really want to be. However, this is great because willpower can be learned. In fact, there are specific ways to increase willpower with practice. Just remember that it doesn't automatically grow. Ultimately it is you who needs to put in the time and practice.

Willpower can otherwise be known as self-discipline, determination, drive and various other names. Essentially willpower is one's ability to resist short term temptations that hurt us in order to succeed at long term goals. When you can avoid unwanted thoughts. When you can stay cool in a hot station. Bodybuilders delay eating that sugary snack until after they have completed the competition. Investors avoid spending on luxuries until they have met their financial goals. Spartans delay resting until they have trained. That's willpower and it's all about delaying gratification.

The motivation to succeed will only get you so far. Watching motivational videos or pumping your state is cool but motivation is something that comes and goes. One day you might feel motivated to conquer the day. But most days you will be far from that feeling. These days it's easier to sit on the couch and just watch TV. Will power is the solution to getting things done. Even when you don't want to.

Having willpower helps us to overcome obstacles and temptations which could lead us astray from our goal. It's the key to freedom. All of us want more freedom and discipline is the key to freedom. Wait, now that might sound kind of counterintuitive. Enforcing restraint and limits on ourselves is the key to freedom? Yes, because you cannot experience true freedom without first having self-discipline. Many times, you need to say no to certain things that steal your freedom. Yet you want to do them because they provide a short-term relief. An escape from the pain. But really, they trap you. Watching pornography for that quick fix is going to trap you in anti-social compulsive behavior. Buying those overpriced shoes that cost more than your monthly paycheck is going to keep you stuck as a wage slave. Clicking social media posts and scrolling through timelines keeps you paralyzed and in a vegetive state. Often, it's instinctive compulsive behavior that you wouldn't really want to do.

How does this equate to more freedom? Think about these examples. A healthy body requires more willpower to exercise and eat right. Having a healthy body is the key to having the freedom to live a fuller and energetic life. A happy relationship can't be that way without working on it and saying no to certain temptations. But that makes the relationship stronger which in turn gives the relationship more freedom of emotions. You can't succeed in business and life without putting the hours in. But that sacrifice ultimately gives you financial freedom when success comes. Discipline to not do those things which disrupt your pathway to success is the key to freedom. More discipline equals more freedom. Everything in life comes at a price. That price is sacrifice and that requires having willpower.

So how do you build more willpower? Begin with setting some rules for your bad habits. Start by making a list of your bad habits. Put them into a table. List the date you last did that habit. List the goal of what you want to do when you're tempted. Put columns for the bad habits, triggers, dates, goals and solutions. For example;

Bad habit	Trigger	Last time	Goal	Solutions
Eating sweets	hunger	15/8	One week no sweets	Make a day where you can indulge. Eat healthy snacks. Don't keep sweets in the house.
Gossip	Jealousy	12/8	No more	Switch topics. Be optimistic. Change your inputs. Change your peers.
Checking socials	boredom	14/8	Limit it	Install blockers. Set time limits.

By having accountability for yourself you're going to be more likely to stick with the plan. Identify what those vices are, and triggers are. After all, our habits are mostly on autopilot so by bringing awareness to them we can work on fixing them. Remember that these aren't rules to burden you but rather to free you. Imagine if you weren't partaking in those bad habits. Stop making excuses. Discover your triggers and find solutions to them. None of us are perfect, we all have bad habits. Don't feel shame or guilt, instead bring the light to the darkness. Then when you complete your goals, reward yourself for it. Long term gratification is much more satisfying.

Form Good Habits & Break Bad Habits

According to habit research it takes roughly sixty days to form new habits. Through repetition neural connections are formed and they get chunked into memory. After enough time habits become woven into a network of actions. When those actions are completed enough times, they become autopilot habits. Usually, we can only focus on building one habit at a time. That is the same both for good and bad habits.

Forming habits requires awareness of your environment and behavior. Essentially it is the process of training your brain to do something without having to stop and think about doing it.

Repetition is the recipe. For example, if you want to exercise every day you get up and do it, repeatedly. To help you create cues. Maybe the cue for exercise is having your gym gear out and ready each day. Or if you want to write more than it's about making it be the first thing you do each morning as you drink your coffee.

Eventually your brain begins to respond to those cues and then trigger those habits. It follows the sequence and order. Much the same as we discussed earlier about bad habits there are triggers to each habit. Therefore, make the most of setting up the right triggers to form good habits. Again, don't try to start too many habits at the same time. It won't work. Go slowly and implement them every few months, one by one. Here are some more great ways of how to form good habits and to make them stick.

Accountability

One of the best ways to get a habit to stick is by having someone hold you accountable for it. Tell your friend or someone you know about a habit you're trying to build. Have a regular call or meeting with them to report on your progress. This will make it more likely to follow through on your plans since you will probably not want to look like a fool to your friend. Imagine being just like the Spartans who had a tribe of warriors holding them accountable for each other.

Switch it out

Maybe your new healthy habit is actually to break a bad habit. That is a tough challenge indeed. Instead, why not try switching that bad habit for something good? Maybe you want to stop eating junk. There is often a behavioral pattern behind that habit. Maybe when you get home after work your natural behavioral pattern is to eat junk food. Instead replace the junk food with some healthy snacks. Fill your fridge up with healthy snacks and get rid of the junk food. After all, you will naturally want to eat a snack when you come home. That's your behavior in action but now you can replace the bad stuff with good stuff. What other bad habits could you switch out? Maybe you could watch motivational videos instead of the times where you indulge in watching gossip or news. Curate your life to default to more healthy options. Adjust your YouTube feed, clean your house and hide the distractions.

Set a timer

Make a deal with yourself if you're struggling to implement a habit. Tell yourself you'll do it for just five or ten minutes. A quick session at the gym. A quick ten minutes on goal setting. Writing one hundred words a day. Whatever it is, start small and try to stick with it. Eventually it then becomes easier, and you end up spending more time on it. Personally, I like to keep charts of my time spent on certain habits. For example, I have a daily word count for writing. I watch the charts grow and that gives me confidence. Or you could have a series of "X" on calendar days for each time you completed your habit.

Write It down

Making a schedule or a plan for your habits makes them more of a priority. Priorities are more important, and we are more likely to stick with them. Write out your plan for the day and put the habit you're working on in there. Plan out your life. That can be a vision which becomes more defined from the whole picture down to the years, months, weeks and days. Continually review it and stick with it. Use your plans to conquer life like the Spartans used theirs to conquer armies.

Reward yourself

Now after all that hard work you deserve a reward. Having a reward for completing habits is also going to provide extra motivation for going after it. Set up some rewards for your hard work. Mark the road with points and rewards along the way to keep you pushing forwards towards successful habits. That could be a cake on a Sunday. A movie night or something fun.

SPARTAN FOCUS & CONCENTRATION

Our senses play an important role in cognitive function and physical health. The sensory system can help you to optimize both mental and physical performance. It is our connection with the outside world. All the time it is sending signals to your brain which consciously and unconsciously decides whether or not it is a positive or negative stimulus. Being mindful of your sensory system can help you to improve focus. In fact, there are some simple techniques that can be used to improve your mental focus.

Athletes are often heard talking about getting in "the zone". It's that state where your focus aligns with your abilities at maximum effect. Imagine the Spartans ready and focused for battle. Concentration is critical to success in business, sports and life. Coming from sports psychology a number of techniques have been identified to help improve your concentration. By definition concentration is about selectively focusing on a single task whilst ignoring irrelevant aspects. Then maintaining attentional focus over time whilst having situational awareness. Consider the definition and think about which parts of it you most struggle with.

One of the most common complaints regarding focus and concentration is brain fog. Otherwise known as subjective memory impairment (SMI) it can happen at any age. Various underlying medical issues can exacerbate the impairment. However, for those practicing healthy living it becomes less of an issue. Now that goes beyond just physical exercise and a good diet.

First of all, the main cause of brain fog is too much multitasking. Are you trying to do too many things at the same time? Thinking of or trying to do too many things at the same time won't get you far. You might think that you're being effective but you're actually going much slower because you're not fully immersed in whatever it is that you're doing. Instead train yourself to focus on just one thing at a time. At first it will be difficult but limit your distractions. Put your electronic devices away whilst working. Block certain websites and put your phone in silent mode.

Confucius says, "The man who chases two rabbits, catches neither."

The next cause of brain fog is overworking. Overworking leads to burnout. Yes, we all want to be Spartan warriors, but the truth is the mind and body need time to recover. It's impossible and ineffective to go full speed, full effort all of the time. Naturally you will burn out. Set aside time for yourself to take a break. Make your breaks revitalizing. For example, go for a walk-in nature. Or have a coffee at your favorite spot. Disconnect. Avoid just being a couch potato. Revitalize. Keep a record of what you're doing each day. Record your exercise and your work. Then you can feel like taking a well-deserved rest or determine when it's best to rest.

Lifestyle factors such as stress, poor sleep, drugs and alcohol can also all lead to brain fog. Apply some simple self-care in your life. Get enough sleep, eat well and avoid toxic inputs. Now if you're still suffering from brain fog after clearing things up then book an appointment with a doctor because there could be a mental condition causing the brain fog.

Improve your focus

Do you want to improve your focus? But perhaps you struggle to know what to focus on. First of all, define the most important factor of what you're doing. For example, when lifting weights, it could be about focusing on your form. Or when studying it could be about having complete attention for a period of time. Maintaining your attention over a period of time can be established by recording the amount of time you succeeded. Record it in a graph or in a diary. Push your limits and get better for longer time periods. Eventually it will become a habit. Furthermore, you can adjust your environment and situations to accommodate better concentration. Maybe that's about turning off electronic devices or going somewhere quiet to get the work done. Find out what is most beneficial to you. Remember this won't happen overnight so stick with it. Cultivate that focused mind.

Develop a Spartan Routine

Spartans had a dedicated structure to their life. This kept the enemies of distraction at bay. With structure they were able to stick to a routine that helped them conquer themselves and eventually their enemies. Routines that included learning, sword fighting, physical training and mental warfare. Much like the Spartans to become a great warrior of life you too will need structure. Discipline as we learned earlier is the ultimate freedom. Start to build structure into your life. Do it on a macro and micro level. Begin with the vision for your life. This is the macro part. What are your ultimate goals and vision for how you want to be remembered? The Spartans will forever be remembered as great warriors. Maybe for you it's about being a great family man. A successful businessman. A musician. A leader. A parent. What's important to you? Define whatever it is.

Next start to break that vision down into small tangible and achievable goals. These should be more specific. Things such as spending time with certain people each week. Metrics for business or whatever it is you're going for. From here you can begin to figure out the important elements of your day. A strongly structured day begins with a solid morning routine. Be in control of your day from the first second. Set your alarm. When it goes off. Wake up. Step into the light and stretch to wake your body up. Drink water. Then start setting your intentions for the day. I recommend writing out your goals, meditating and planning first. No checking social media or watching TV. Those will just distract you. Recently I had an example of how this can really screw up your day. Three days earlier I had booked a flight ticket. A few days later I checked my phone in the morning. This was an autopilot mistake. Upon checking I saw that I had been double charged for the airline ticket. This set into motion screwing up my day as I wasted the first few hours chasing up airlines. Ultimately, I didn't get any result until much later into the evening. Would have been better to not check until later on. Really it was not urgent.

Preserve your mornings. There is nothing more urgent than taking care of your routine. Willpower is at its peak in the morning so make the most of that. After completing your morning routine, start work on your most important task for the day. If you have a job, then that's going to be determined more by this commitment. But you should still establish some control and priority setting there. For me I like to first make a rough plan for the day. Plan your days, weeks, months and life. Long term it will be more of a vision and on a shorter term you can go into the finer details.

Usually, the first task of the day for me is writing for one to two hours or learning something. This depends on which is more important at that period in my life. I then like to take a break to recharge. Perhaps that's going for a walk to buy a coffee or having some lunch. At this point it's fine to reply to some messages. You've completed some important tasks already. Just don't get too caught up in the non-essential things. The following part of your day should still stick within some structure. Set aside chunks of time to work undistracted on high priory activities. Set aside time to exercise. Set aside time to learn. At the end of the day set aside time to play, unwind and spend time with loved ones. Then you can do some of the non-essentials and have some fun.

SPARTAN FEARLESSNESS

Ever since the beginning of time fear has been around. Inside of all living creatures is fear. The main purpose of it is to keep us alive and safe when faced with danger. Our brains default to fear because it is a primal human emotion. One of the first emotions expressed by man was fear. Adam said to God,

"I heard you in the garden, and I was afraid because I was naked; so, I hid'.

Our natural tendency as humans is to lean towards fear. But just as the scriptures detailed men and women of fear they also showed them how to overcome fear. Indeed, fear can be very useful when we are faced with dangers. However, through evolution we have also developed a fear of dangers that exist only in our minds. Incidentally those are fears that might never even happen. For the most part these can often be rather unrealistic. In fact, it is fear which holds us back from many of our goals and the success we deserve. Those fears of failures, success, not being good enough, rejection and so on. All of us live with this. Fear won't go away so we have to learn to deal with it.

"The wolf begins to circle the boy. Claws of black steel, fur as dark night. Eyes glowing red, jewels from the pit of hell itself. The giant wolf sniffing savored the scent of the meal to come. It's not fear that grips him, only a heightened sense of things."
300

King Leonidas overcame his fears. The giant wolf was a fright for sure. But he did not wrestle with that fear. He was aware of it. He faced it. He had faith in himself. Faith to overcome fear. He acted regardless of fear. Fear heightened his senses and brought power into his thrust of the spear which slayed the giant wolf.

Merriam-Webster defines fear as: "an unpleasant often strong emotion caused by anticipation or awareness of danger"

Recently Brazilian Jiu-Jitsu legend Rickson Gracie who was undefeated in his martial arts career talked about when he first encountered fear. In his first bout as an 80kg nineteen-year-old he faced a huge opponent, Reii Zulu. Zulu was over 100kg and had a record of about two hundred victories and two draws. No defeats. It really was a case of David versus the giant goliath. Late into the second round Rickson wanted to quit. But his father told him not to. In the break his brother threw ice water over him which shocked him into alertness. He then went on to submit Zulu. After the fight Rickson recounted that he swore to never let his mind defeat him again. To never let fear, determine his fate. Later he asked his brother to roll him up in a carpet for over ten minutes in the summer heat. He was essentially being suffocated in extreme heat. This act helped him to get comfortable with his fear.

Now you don't need to wrap yourself up in a carpet to conquer fear, but you will need to get accustomed with fear. So how do you overcome fear? First of all, do not run away from it. Your human instinct will be to first retreat from scary situations. But that won't help you. Note, unless there is a life and death situation. In that case don't let pride get in the way. For example, if someone holds a gun to your head and asks for your money don't fight, give it to them. Money is replaceable but life is priceless. Don't risk your life because of pride or something replaceable. Now let's be clear what we are talking about is the fear that stands in the way of getting what you want. Fears such as asking that girl out. Fears such as travelling to a new place. Fears such as trying something new and so on. Fears that stop you doing what you really want to.

Say hello to your fear and acknowledge it. Feel that fear. Practice mindful awareness so that you can sit with that fear, observe it and experience it. Your sweaty palms, fast heartbeat, anxiety and so on. Whenever fear comes up, recognize it. Realize that it's a feeling. You can get used to it and not be bothered by it anymore. A famous saying goes like this. Keep your friends close and your enemies closer. Have the same approach to fear. Learn to get comfortable with it and accept it.

"Fear is like fire. You can make it work for you: it can warm you in winter, cook your food when you're hungry, give you light when you are in the dark, and produce energy. Let it go out of control and it can hurt you, even kill you... Fear is a friend of exceptional people``. - Cus d'amato - legendary boxing trainer of Muhamid Ali, Mike Tysom and many more.

As you begin to notice your fears you can then apply some tactics to it. Start with small steps. Commit to doing something fearful for a short period of time. Or to take a small step towards it. For example, commit to going up a few more floors each time if heights scare you. Or if confrontation scares you try sparring at a professional gym. Practice getting into those fearful situations more and desensitizing yourself to them. Eventually you will notice that it is your mind which makes things much worse than they really are.

Again, start small with those actions and build yourself up. Keep going for it and stay consistent. In time you will grow stronger. Remember that your human and fear is normal. All of us are afraid of something. Some fears are easier to notice than others. It's important that you acknowledge your fears. Don't be in denial about them otherwise they will come up and much worse later on. Make a list of your fears and how you would overcome them. Make a list of the fears that are holding you back. By identifying and acknowledging them you can start to work on overcoming them.

Courage

Courage is the mastery of fear. Courage recognizes fear but allows you to be with it and go past it. Brave warriors still feel fear. Spartans still feel fear. But the difference between them and the ones who run away from it is courage. The brave feel fear but they still go for it regardless. The Spartans undoubtedly faced fear at The Battle of Thermopylae when confronted with a giant Persian army. Yet they went for it and attacked. They went all in until death because they had courage and mastery of their emotions.

Face your demons and stand up to them. Maybe you fear rejection, but you tell someone you love them anyway. That's courage. Or maybe you are uncertain of your future, but you know you deserve better, so you quit your job. Again, that's courage. start working on building more courage. Otherwise, you will keep defaulting to that primal human fear.

As we know now fear is always there hanging around. It's part of our biology. Realize fear and you can deal with it. Because if you hide from it, it grows. Then it makes it harder to confront it. Learn to be present with fear and use courage to move you forwards. Start taking chances. Take on those new projects. Try new approaches and express yourself. Show up to life. Be ok with making mistakes. That will happen. Just learn from it. Doesn't matter if you fail. Focus on being brave and courageous like a Spartan!

SPARTAN BODY

So, you want to look ripped, lean and muscular like a Spartan? Getting to that level is going to require a strong mindset. But you've learned all about that! Now it's time to start getting physical with some of the good food and workouts. In this chapter you will find all of that. The focus here will be on simple bodyweight exercises and basic non processed foods. After all, the Spartans didn't have access to modern fancy gyms or protein shakes. Yet they built incredible bodies. Therefore, so can you.

Master your mornings

The mornings will become the most important part of your physical routine. Begin your mornings with some short bursts of exercise. You can try one of the following and alternate them on different days of the week. Make a rest day on Sunday because rest is important to allow your body time to recover.

Morning exercise examples

Choose one for each morning and alternate them:

- Up to four rounds of five minutes of shadow boxing or boxing with a bag. Rest for one minute in between each round. Total time is twenty minutes.

- One hundred push-ups and one hundred sit ups. You can break these down into sets.

- A twenty to thirty-minute light jog. This can be done on a treadmill or outdoors. As you prefer.

*Meditation - be sure to meditate every morning. First thing is the best. No apps, just focus your breathing.

Cardio

Perform at least one hundred and fifty to two hundred minutes of cardio each week. You can include the morning exercises as part of those cardio minutes. Now don't make all of your cardio intense. No HIT stuff here. Save that energy for the calisthenics and bodyweight routines. One week you can build up from one hundred fifty minutes and the next week go up to one hundred seventy-five. Then two hundred for the next week. Then cycle back down. Cardio can be done morning and evening. Just hit your minutes each week.

Cardio examples

- Cycling

- Sprints

- Martial arts

- Jogging

- Surfing

- Climbing

- Brisk walking

Muscle building

Since the Spartans didn't have the luxury of modern gyms these workouts won't either. Instead, they will focus on calisthenic bodyweight exercises. In fact, these are incredibly effective. At first you will probably find them to be extremely difficult. That's because it's a new way of exercising but in fact it is an ancient time-tested method of building lean, muscular and brutal bodies. Start each workout with some stretches to warm your muscles up. Google images search the following if you're not sure how they look.

Stretch out

Hold these positions for up to four breaths and cycle through them two to three times. They should warm up your body and give you a nice energy boost. Examples:

- Touch your toes and fold over. Hold it for four breaths.

- Split your legs out and reach down to the ground.

- Perform a downward facing dog pose. Hold it and flex side to side.

- Perform a child pose. Move around your shoulders.

- Perform a warrior one and warrior two pose. Hold it for four breaths.

- Sit cross legged or with one leg extended. The other one should be flexed and near you. Lean to stretch around you - it's like a twisting movement.

- Swivel your hips. Four swivels each direction.

- Stretch each leg out one by one. Lean over to each side and touch your toes.

- Lay on your back and push your hips up. Hold it for four breaths.

- Lay on your back and cross a leg over one side. Perform the stretch both ways.

Muscle building exercises

Now for the muscle building exercises. Beginners can perform these workouts with just one set per exercise. Advanced people can perform them for up to five sets. Each week try performing more sets. Keep a record of your gym log. Remember don't have your phone out during the workouts. The Spartans did not have phones, they had full focus. So be fully present and in the moment. Focus on your body. Now here are the workouts. They focus on body parts each day. You can cycle through them each week. Go for four to six workouts a week. Then take a rest day.

Chest workout

First warm up the chest. Then perform the following.

1. Push-ups - perform 10 to 20 reps - add weight if you can (stones or water bottles are good)

2. Ring dip or something with similar structure - perform 8 to 15 reps - add weight if you can.

3. Incline push up (feet raised on a surface) - perform 10 to 20 reps - add weight if you can.

4. Incline ring dip or something with a similar structure - perform 8 to 15 reps - add weight if you can.

5. Decline push up (hands higher up) - perform 10 to 20 reps - add weight if you can.

Back and abs workout

First warm up the back. Then perform the following.

1. Crunch - perform 15 to 25 reps.

2. Plank - hold for 45 to 70 seconds. Add weight if you can.

3. Mountain climbers - perform 20 to 25 reps.

4. Pull ups - work until failure. Add weight if you can.

5. Prone cobra - perform 5 to 10 reps.

6. Bodyweight rear delt fly - perform 15 to 20 reps.

7. Inverted rows - perform 15 to 20 reps.

8. Suspension bodyweight rows or band pull aparts - perform 5 to 10 reps.

Shoulders workout

First warm up the shoulders. Then perform the following.

1. Wall walk - perform one to five times.

2. Handstand holds - learn how to safely do this first. I suggest Chris Heira tutorials on YouTube.

3. Muscle ups - learn to safely do one first and then try to do more. Again, look at some tutorials on YouTube. This is an advanced movement. 5 to 10 reps.

4. Bear crawl - crawl 10 meters per set.

5. Pike push-ups - perform 10 to 15 reps.

Arms workout

First warm up the arms. Then perform the following.

1. Box dips - perform 5 to 10 reps.

2. Chin ups - perform 5 to 10 reps. Add weight if you can.

3. Diamond push-ups - perform 5 to 10 reps.

4. Inverted rows with underhand grip - perform 10 to 15 reps.

5. Pull ups with inverted grip and slow release (go fast up and slowly downwards) - perform 5 to 10 reps.

6. Dips - perform 5 to 10 reps. Add weight if you can.

Legs and abs workout

First warm up the legs. Then perform the following.

1. Air squats - perform 10 to 15 reps. Add weight if you can.

2. One leg squat - perform 5 to 10 reps per side. Add weight if you can.

3. Lunges - perform 5 to 10 reps per side. Add weight if you can.

4. Glute bridge - perform 5 to 10 reps. Add weight if you can.

5. Step ups - perform 10 to 20 reps. Add weight if you can.

6. Burpees - perform 5 to 10 reps.

7. Side crunches - perform 15 to 20 reps per side.

8. Leg raises - perform 10 to 20 reps.

Diet

The Spartan diet outlined here focuses on the concepts of intermittent fasting combined with a paleo diet. Intermittent fasting is about eating your meals within a set window of time suitable for you. Usually that's to stop eating four hours before bed. Then sleep eight hours and have your next meal four hours after waking. That is a total of sixteen hours fasting. The process of fasting will give your digestive system adequate rest, shred fat and in turn give you a lean body. Additionally, your mental toughness will be strengthened through the adversity of fasting. Figure out your bedtime and wake up time. Then implement intermittent fasting around those times. You can even try day fasts if you want. Just be sure to drink plenty of water and do not overdo things during the fast.

As for the paleo diet this is a diet focused on the times before we had processed foods. Times such as when the Spartans were around. Basically, it's about eating clean unprocessed food. Low sugars, low carbs and high protein. High protein content will help to build strong muscles. So, eat plenty of steaks, boiled vegetables, lean meats and so on. Nothing processed, fried or filled with additives. Simple and clean natural food. Here are some examples of what to eat and when.

Breakfast

Eat breakfast after your fasting time - so it could actually be in the afternoon.

- Oatmeal with water (avoid milk)

- Banana or some fruits

- Scrambled egg whites (less fat)

Lunch

It's good to wait at least two hours before your next meal. Let your digestion do its work.

- Chicken breast or fish

- Broccoli or some greens

- Sweet potatoes - a great source of clean energy

Pre workout

Don't eat too much here because it will make you sluggish during your workout.

- Banana or two

- Black coffee

Dinner

You worked out hard so have yourself a nice hearty dinner.

- Steak around 200 grams

- Rice or potatoes

- Spinach and vegetables

Last snack

Have a light snack before bed. Your body should be relaxed when sleeping. Not digesting a ton of food.

- Nuts (a couple of handfuls)

- Fruits

- Eggs

That should be plenty of food. If you feel it's not enough and you're losing too much weight or not having enough energy, then by all means add more or shrink your fasting window. If it's too much, then do the opposite. Overall, you should feel like you have plenty of energy and not feel bloated. This diet and method enhance that. It's energy for life. Stick with the same meals each week. That is again a practice of discipline which will set you free. Free because you won't have to spend hours thinking about what to eat. Instead, you can save that mental energy for something more important. Plus, you can make use of the amazing energy these natural foods will give you.

SPARTAN LIFE PRINCIPLES

The Spartans followed some very powerful life principles. In this chapter you are going to discover some of those. These life principles have been distilled and revised based on who the Spartans were and how they lived. Make use of those principles found here to help enhance your life.

Give everything

Returning home alive from a lost battle was the greatest shame for a Spartan. Finish everything that you start. That means you should only start something if you are sure that you can finish it. Being a finisher will make you a more effective person this way. Commit to your goals and go all in on them. Slay through them. Do your best and give three hundred percent!

Stay lean and hungry

Consume only plain food and do not eat to the point of satisfaction. Eat healthy and you will become what you eat. Eat good and feel good. Use food as fuel. Spartans ate this way. Eggs for breakfast is a great start to the day. Add in plenty of vegetables throughout the day. Get enough proteins, fibers and low sugars. If you eat snacks, go healthy. Furthermore, incorporate intermittent fasting into your routine. Where you eat only for eight hours a day. The rest you fast. It will make you lean and disciplined. Never overeat, it will make you a sloth. Stay hungry for more from life.

Seek out competition that is intense

Every Spartan aimed to push himself harder both mentally and physically so that once the trial was completed they would become better. Continuously introduce yourself to tough situations where you are forced to either sink or swim. Learn to quickly adapt. Don't get comfortable with any plateaus you're facing. Push through them. Challenge yourself. One of the best ways is by working out. Have someone there to push you to do more. Or it could be taking on goals bigger than you're comfortable with. Expect to succeed and you will figure it out. Don't be afraid to get dirty and grind out the hard work.

Accept death

Spartans accepted death so that they could live courageously and free themselves from the limits of fear. Now don't get this wrong. No this isn't about standing in traffic as a fool. Or risking your life. Actually, it's about being willing to go after what you want and to not be scared. Face your fears head on as an adult. Revisit the chapter about fear again and again to help you to get comfortable with fear.

Do not gossip

Spartans focused only on conversations that nourished the soul and strengthened their spirit. They were a united people. Gossiping about others is a vicious circle. If you're a gossip, then you can very well expect others to gossip about you as do about them. Instead of talking about others, talk about your dreams, accomplishments and plans. Seek out people who share the same ideas. Avoid others who engage in gossip.

Fight for a good cause

Spartans fought to protect Sparta. To face off the invaders who wanted to crush them. Choose your battles wisely. Don't waste your time on things that just aren't worth it. You only have so much time available each day. Spend it wisely and go all in on what you're doing. One thing at a time. Mastery. This will push you to go further and defend your honor.

Surround yourself with the greatest

Spartans built strong armies of warriors who were devoted to becoming their best. Be like them. Surround yourself with others who want to become better. Surround yourself with others who are better than you. If you're the smartest in the room, then you're in the wrong room. Look to others to inspire you and lift each other up to greater heights. Like the Spartans, listen to your elders and those who are wiser.

Lead from the front

Great leaders don't watch safely from the sidelines. The great king Leonidas led the 300 hundred Spartans into an epic battle. He led by example and fought at the front lines. Be like him. Get your hands dirty. Learn how to do difficult tasks and then outsource them. First you have to grind it out, build steel and become a conqueror. Maybe that's about putting your hand up first to volunteer. Or it could even be the one to show up first at work. Live like how you want others to.

Follow structure and organization

Spartans were notorious for their tough training. Rigorous structure and organization were followed to build strong warriors. Nowadays it's become easy to be led astray by all the distractions. Often the biggest battle is on the inside. Plan ahead for those times when you could get distracted. Schedule your time. From the years to the months. Then fill up your days and live them to the fullest.

Refuse to be a victim

Every Spartan was responsible for themselves, and they were loyal to their comrades. Being a victim was an act of cowardice. They had to own their battles and be responsible for victory. Learn to rely on yourself, take responsibility and be prepared for anything. Crying over what happened to you or the current situation will get you nowhere. Stand up and do something about it. Make moves or make excuses.

"Leaders must own everything in their world. There is no one

else to blame." — Jocko Willink

Master discomfort

We have talked a lot about mastering discomfort. When Spartans went into battle, they had to deal with the discomfort of being away from their families in faraway foreign lands. But the battles were worth the victory.

Introduce short periods of discomfort into your daily life. It will prevent you from becoming lazy. Do hard things. The easy times are good, but we should only enjoy them after some accomplishment. The tough times shape us and create our stories. The more difficult those times are, the more strength there is to be gained. Life in the modern world has become far too comfortable and easy. We get complacent and it's ok to have noodles every day and watch reruns on Netflix. But my friend, that's not good for you. That base level of comfort needs to be overcome. Take on big goals and strive for more. Challenge yourself. Yes, that will require some discomfort. But deal with it and get over it. Try to build character through challenges such as sleeping on your floor, taking cold showers or eating basic meals.

Commit to lifelong learning

Become a lifetime learner. There is an infinite amount of knowledge out there. Just because you graduated, learning doesn't stop there. The Spartans were learning every day and improving their training. They learned the long and hard way. They sought advice from their elders. Eventually they would become wise like them. Keep learning about your business, culture, life and more. It's not just about books. Take courses, find mentors, travel and get experience to learn from.

Know thyself

The Ancient Greek saying "know thyself" was written at the Temple of Apollo. Spartans ultimately had to learn about themselves. They had to know how to be stronger and less weak. Inside of us there is often a polarity between good and evil. Learn what your vices and weaknesses are. Know what causes you troubles and temptations. Know what brings the best from you.

Socrates — 'To know thyself is the beginning of wisdom.'

Set a standard for yourself

Spartan armies were famous for overpowering much larger ones. Maybe one Spartan was worth hundreds of enemy soldiers. They lived up to such high standards to become this way. Their high-level training made this possible. Remember that you're the one who is in control of your destiny. Whether you believe it or not everything you do and think shapes it. Find your purpose in life and work hard for it. Those who do this will succeed the most. Do not accept anything which you feel is below you. Hold out for something better and it will come. Belief and patience will bring it to you.

Never surrender

The Spartans were famous for never surrendering. Even when defeat looked certain at the battle of Thermopylae they never surrendered. Death was inevitable but to them death was an honor. Now don't take this literally. In modern times you don't need to die for a cause. But what it does mean is that you shouldn't give up when the going gets tough. When you start a new project, it might seem like you're going nowhere. Keep pushing through. Remember you're often just three feet from gold. Work on having more grit. It's the power to come back from failure. Spartans always come back for more. Remember to never surrender

CONCLUSION

In this book you have discovered life lessons and knowledge from the Spartan warriors. Forever they have gone down in history as legends. Their wisdom, courage and power remain eternal, made famous in the battle of 300 Spartans at Thermopylae. Remember that it is a legacy of mortals and that is possible for you too. Even though this all happened thousands of years ago, and we no longer die by the sword. Those lessons that they left behind are still valuable. They have been distilled into this book as something that you can still use in modern life.

As I mentioned at the start of this book, we live in a very comfortable world where in recent times most of us have been confined to our own homes. Safe from an invisible enemy. It's almost like we have been wrapped up in cotton wool. We're having food delivered to our door and life on demand. You can stay in bed all day and that's just fine. But that's a below average life and it's not going to make you happy. In fact, most people are becoming depressed, having mental issues and pacifying in negative ways. The problem with this life is that there's no initiation, no right of way or life lessons that help us. That's the truth of the matter. But the Spartans were not escaping struggles and there's a lot that we can learn from them. Lessons from them can help us to become stronger. Indeed, the times we live in are different, but they are still times that present us with challenges.

Spartan history gives us insights into the ways they lived and the times that they lived in. Learning about this helps us to understand how those times affected their training and lifestyles which turned them into powerful warriors. The most famous part of their history was the battle of Thermopylae where 300 Spartans faced off in battle against a much larger Persian army. Even though they lost the battle it cemented their legacy as they gave the Persians hell. Their training methods and lifestyles which instilled virtues of strength, endurance and fearlessness helped them to achieve this incredible feat.

With an understanding of their history and lives we explored Spartan mental toughness. Nowadays the Spartan's seem almost mythical. How were they able to fight off such huge armies? Were they really human? Yes, they were, and it was primarily mental toughness that helped them achieve insurmountable feats. You too can develop mental toughness by conditioning yourself to embrace discomfort on a frequent basis. This is going to allow you to push past boundaries and as a result grow stronger. That's what Spartan training and life principles were all about. They are all about pushing your boundaries and in this chapter, you can find exercises to help you cultivate those mindsets and to overcome challenges. Mostly it's a focus on being more accustomed to the tougher aspects of life which will in turn make you a stronger person.

In the next chapter we took a look at Spartan willpower. Such willpower helped them to deal with living in a harsh world and to be ready for the enemy at any time. We too can learn and adapt willpower to our own lives so that we're not always tempted by things that make us weak. Will power help us to focus on the right things and to avoid the bad situations. We learned that will power is in fact something that can be practiced and learned. In this particular chapter we explored some keyways to build more willpower. Motivation is only going to get you so far and willpower is the ultimate solution towards long-term success instead of short-term gratification. Incidentally that's going to give you more freedom because you'll be free from the vices and distractions which take you away from your destiny. Furthermore, we looked at how to break good bad habits and form good ones. In short, those methods include how your environment, accountability and other methods can help you to implement good habits.

Moving on to the next chapter we explored Spartan focus and concentration. This world we're living in right now is chaotic. That's an understatement! Issues such as brain fog are affecting our ability to deal with life and make things happen. Thousands of years ago the Spartan era was much simpler. Naturally they had more focus and concentration. We too need to be able to implement that kind of simplicity into our lives. Distraction free lives will allow us to improve our cognitive function and physical health. We need to be able to cultivate a calmer mind and to not multitask or burn out. We need to be able to concentrate better which will help us in business, health and life. Spartan life structures can help us to keep the distractions away. Much like them we need structure and simplicity to free us from distractions and to focus on what's important. Explore this chapter again to build a more concentrated and disciplined mind.

Onto the next chapter we explored Spartan fearlessness. The Spartans were famous for their fearlessness. However, they were humans just like us. They felt fear just like us. But they had the courage to sit with their fears and to do what they wanted regardless of fear. Fear has been around since the beginning of time as a way of trying to keep us alive. But most of the time it keeps us from living the life we really want. This chapter explores how to deal with fear and to become a more courageous person. Courage is the mastery of fear, and it will allow you to recognize fear but go past it. Make the most of the exercises and knowledge presented here to become courageous like a Spartan.

The Spartans were famous for having strong and powerful ripped bodies. In the next chapter we explore how to build bodies just like them. The methods here focused on simple exercises because Spartans did not have access to modern gyms. Therefore, these workouts focused on core exercises, calisthenics, body weight and a simple diet. No need for high tech gyms or fad diets. Stick with the information in this chapter and you too will look and feel like a Spartan.

In the last chapter we took a look at Spartan life principles.

These are distilled based on how they lived. I recommend that you revisit this chapter often because it is probably the most important one in this whole book. The Spartans gave everything and returning home alive from a battle was a great shame for them. Learn from them. Don't ever leave anything on the table and go all in on this life. Build a strong mindset that's going to allow you to deal with the challenges of life. Embrace discomfort and get comfortable with it. Get to know yourself, your weaknesses and your strengths. Make your fears your best friends. Fight for a good cause and surround yourself with the best people. Warriors who have the same mindsets and who can lift you up to becoming a better person. Never, ever be a victim. Be the one that's responsible for your life. A life that has structure and organization. Be the one who is committed to lifelong learning.

Destiny is waiting for you. Set goals that seem so huge. Be like the Spartans who faced off against a gigantic Persian army. Never surrender and believe in yourself. Even when it seems impossible. Yes, because you deserve much more and you can get much better than you think. Fight and hold out for it. Strive to become the greatest and live your life like a Spartan warrior. You see they were born with nothing in a harsh world thousands of years ago. But that didn't mean they would become no one. Just like them I hope that what you've learned in this book can help you to become a better person. A person that can overcome the challenges of life in the pursuit of goals to get what you want for yourself and much more. That could be in business, your personal life, health or wherever you wish to improve. By building a better mindset and living the way of the Spartan you'll become a stronger and better person for this life. That will free you to live a better life. A life that will go down in history forever.

That's the way of the Spartan.

OVERTHINKING

---

*HOW TO STOP OVERTHINKING,
ESCAPE NEGATIVE THOUGHTS,
DECLUTTER YOUR MIND, RELIEVE
STRESS & ANXIETY, BUILD MENTAL
TOUGHNESS & LIVE FULLY*

THOMAS SWAIN

INTRODUCTION

Thoughts travel faster than anything on planet earth.

They are limitless in potential and can change in an instant. According to scientific data the brain can store around a million gigabytes and make more than a trillion connections through over one billion neurons. This equates to storing over three million hours of video or letting a movie run for over three hundred years in full high definition. Now that's just the storage capacity of the brain. Then there is the processing capacity of it. Human brains are far superior at processing than even the most advanced computers. Computers require millions of steps to calculate something which can be achieved using just a few hundred transmissions of brain neurons. Plus, humans can make advanced plans, decisions and understand morality and humor.

Our superiority in cognitive ability and capacity sets us apart from the other animals on planet earth. However, it is this same brain power that leaves us susceptible to overthinking. Taming such powerful brains to think clearly and calmly can be troublesome. Overthinking is a common issue. There are two forms of overthinking, worrying about the future or ruminating about the past. Bad scenarios play out in their head like a hurricane of problems. Past troubles haunt them, and the future burdens worry them. Even though most of these things never happened or it was never as bad as they imagined. Yet it still nags at them. Overthinkers tend to be very unrealistic and overly pessimistic. When things happen that they don't expect it can rock them and things can often get dark

"I can't stop thinking," or "I wish I had done this, or I wish life was like that".

On and on it goes...

All of us can be affected by overthinking. We worry about our love life, our work life, our day-to-day responsibilities, the decisions we made in the past and so on. Essentially, we are not in full control of our thoughts. Rather it is our thoughts that are controlling us. This can build up to unwanted negative results and a dimmer overall outlook on life. All of this of course has a ton of harmful side effects. Here are just a few of them.

- Difficulty to have normal conversations because you overthink how people will receive you.

- Constantly comparing yourself to others and feeling worse because you don't match up to them.

- Obsession over bad events that never happened.

- Stuck in the past, dwelling on your mistakes.

- Worrying about your future and doubting your abilities to succeed.

- Thoughts overwhelm you leading to worry, stress and anxiety.

Now is overthinking really a problem? I know what you're thinking (excuse the pun here). But I need to think? Thinking is a superpower of humans. Einstein thought about developing the theory of relativity. Newton thought about gravity. Elon Musk thinks about rockets and Justin Bieber thinks about music. Incidentally overthinking is ok. That's as long as you are aware of and in control of where your thoughts are going. The mind requires a solid foundation and establishing boundaries will help it to grow in the right direction. Those boundaries could come in limiting time to thinking, avoiding certain pathways such as negativity or focusing on a particular thing and nothing else.

Life becomes more enjoyable when you stop overthinking. When your mind is freer from the chains of overthinking it gives you the time and space to enjoy life. Without the mind-numbing endless decisions, you will inevitably make more positive things happen. Then you can spend time actually living life instead of just thinking about it or what might happen. Inner peace arises and your mind becomes free of worries, fears or regrets about the past or just mindless thoughts. Opportunities and joy will be abundant to you when you are more in the moment. All it takes is quieting the chatter of your mind. That can be done with ease.

Where does overthinking come from?

The human brain essentially is programmed to keep you alive and safe from prehistoric predators. Overthinking originates from the emotional part of your brain which is one of our primal preservation instincts. It is a speculative tool that will mostly analyze the worst possible perspective as a method of protecting you. Although it's not really beneficial in our modern world. For those of us who are more prone to overthinking this part of our brain is much more active. We tend to focus on the worst-case scenarios because our brain is responding in a flight or fight mode. This mode exacerbates feelings of helplessness, stress and anxiety.

Imagine how it all plays out in the real world. Say you're working in a busy office and your boss asks you to try out a new reporting method. But you don't like it. So, you explain why it's a bad idea to the boss. A debate spreads throughout the office. Suddenly you're to blame for the distraction and delay. But you didn't do anything wrong? You go home and think about what happened that day. In fact, you think about it all night and it keeps you awake. Maybe your boss will fire you. Maybe your colleagues will hate you. Maybe it's time you find a new job. Maybe you should hand in your resignation notice tomorrow. At least you won't get fired. But maybe your boss is grateful for you highlighting this.

Going over this scenario is exhausting and most of these highly imagined scenarios will not even come true.

Each person has their own individual reasons for overthinking. Those depend on our own internal make up and our own life. That being said, there are some common themes to consider. In brief, here are some of the main reasons. We will explore them and their solutions in more detail later on.

Stress

When our mind is frantically seeking solutions, it causes stress. The positive part of stress is that it is a result of real problems. That means those have real solutions. Therefore, eventually those problems can be resolved and in turn escape the hold of overthinking. The difference between anxiety and stress is that anxiety does not have any logical or real-world causes.

Anxiety

Anxiety is a leading cause of overthinking. The NHS recently reported that one in five adults in the UK suffer from generalized anxiety disorder (GAD). Often it begins with logic, but this often spirals into much less logical directions. Like a fire burning hotter the more you think about it the more it grows. Anxiety and overthinking are very closely linked. We fail to live in the present moment but get anxious about the past or future worries.

Depression

Excessive overthinking creates feelings of distress that can lead to depression. This also goes the other way. A depressed person often is overthinking how bad things are. They ruminate and the thoughts cycle around their minds. It can lead to regret, self-loathing and blame. Rumination is usually a catalyst of developing depression.

Decision making

Many of us struggle when it comes to making decisions. We feel it's normal to think in detail about decisions. But at what point does it become irrational to overthink decisions? Well that all depends on the context. Every day we are presented with decisions. From what food to eat to bigger decisions such as who to marry or what company to work for and so on. Indeed, some decisions do require more thought. But it should be a deliberate and active way of thinking. Thinking that we might make a wrong choice can be paralyzing. It is a difficult road to navigate. Most people get stuck here because they fear failure or being wrong. Overthinking small decisions will lead us astray. Instead of taking action and sticking with a decision the overthinker breaks it apart and down into an intellectual debate. Something simple ends up becoming quite complex. The failure of overthinking is that it prevents real thinking from taking place. Instead, there is a swarm of ideas and scenarios going around without any real meaning.

Information Overload

Our modern high-tech world everyday overwhelms us with new stimuli. But it is also an exciting one that should be lived with joy. Music, television, social media and so many other sources offer us an abundance of information that is accessible at any time. Never before have we been able to curate our world like this. Think about it, in the not-too-distant past we had to watch whatever show was on at that particular time. Back then there were limited choices as to how we spent our time and as such there was much less to think about. Nowadays we have so many choices that simple decisions such as deciding what to eat can create brain overload. Stuck in thought we are left unable to live fully.

Such an energetic and abundant world can be an overwhelming place. The overthinking person feels, sees and hears everything much more. Fine details of life overfill their minds and memories. Thoughts are broken down to the smallest of details. Too much is going on. Too much to process and too much inevitably leads to burnout, anxiety and stress. Life becomes difficult to process and the results end up even more overwhelming. This is the trap of overthinking, and it goes on like water swirling down a sinkhole, speeding up and out of control.

"It's not a daily increase, but a daily decrease. Hack away at the inessentials."

– Bruce Lee

Negativity Bias

For millions of years the human nervous system evolved to what it is today. But it has remained the same as when we were at the risk of being faced with man-eating predators. That same response to keep us safe and alive tends to overestimate threats and underestimate opportunities. This is known as the negativity bias and is essentially our human default to react more intensely to the negative than the positive. In terms of thinking it causes us to overthink and worry more than is necessary. We are no longer a primitive cave species. The modern world is a far safer place.

Insomnia

Picture the scene. You're in bed ready to sleep but you're still wide awake. You think, "I have just eight hours to sleep before work." So, you check your phone, scroll through some notifications and one more hour has passed. But you still haven't slept a wink. Thoughts start to crowd your mind. Round and round the thoughts go. This makes you obsessed which makes you more tired but unable to sleep because your mind just won't switch off.

Mental Health Conditions

As you can see there are a multitude of reasons for overthinking. Each individual has their own triggers and reasons. Then there are some which are the result of medical and health conditions. Those include obsessive-compulsive disorder (OCD) or General Anxiety Disorder (GAD). More serious long-term depression can also be a type of mental illness that causes over thinking. If you suffer from such conditions, please seek medical advice or contact a mental health professional.

Presenting solutions

Realize that you are in control of your own thoughts and actions. Indeed, sometimes a little bit of worry about the future or reflection on the past is healthy. That can help us become better. The difference between that and overthinking is that the latter is more passive than active. Awareness of your overthinking is the first step to making a change. When you recognize that it does you more harm than good then you're on your way to a positive evolution. Indeed, we can change outcomes of future events happening. But we can't imagine that into reality. Instead of thinking about it, we actually need to take action. Ready, aim fire. It's all a quick sequence. Remind yourself that you cannot control other people. You cannot change what they think or do. They are the ones in control of themselves.

Don't despair and think there is nothing you can do from here. This book was written specifically to solve your overthinking. In fact, there are several exercises and mindsets that will help you to escape overthinking. First, we will take a look at the causes. Then we will look at some of the ways you can upgrade your thinking. From self-esteem to mindfulness, mental toughness and much more. In the conclusion we will explore the promises made and summarize the key points.

My name is Thomas Swain. Like millions of others, I struggled and failed in search of success and happiness. Growing up I had a blurred vision of my goals in life. I thought money, fame and success would be the answer. Yet I was unsatisfied. I struggled with insomnia and stress. Through the ups and downs, I found peace of mind in the concepts outlined in this book. A common struggle of many people right now. I promise you to overthink can be healed. In this book allow me to outline some of the ways and we will work on it together. With consistency in your practice your mind will become calmer and less likely to spiral out of control.

Let us make sure our thinking is useful to us. When thinking, let's aim for clarity and control. Recognize when we get stuck in anxiety and confusion. Seek help from others and be forgiving of yourself. Don't avoid the pain points. Look at the negatives and how you can work on making them positives.

Now let us harness our super brain power!

EXPLORING THE REASONS FOR OVERTHINKING

Every person has their own individual reasons for overthinking. Those depend on our genetic makeup, our own life circumstances and the events that shape us. That being said, there are some common reasons to consider. Let's take a look and explore them in this chapter. In the next chapter we will explore solutions to them. But first to be effective and break free from overthinking we need to understand the reasons behind it.

Stress

Stress is a part of everyday life. It is how our body responds to pressure by releasing the stress hormones of cortisol and adrenaline. Life events can trigger us to feel more or less of this pressure. Unfortunately, there is not really a universal medical definition of what stress is. Because of this, health care professionals often disagree as to whether or not stress causes certain problems or is the result of them. Naturally this makes it difficult to identify stress and resolve it.

Truth is that we all feel stressed sometimes. It can even motivate or help us. For the success driven person, it can often become a way of life. Our ability to cope is unique to each of us. It depends on our genetics, life experience and circumstances. But for other people, the things we can cope with might overwhelm them. In the worst case it can negatively affect a person's life resulting in many unwanted effects both physically and mentally.

When you're constantly stressed out it can become a serious health issue. Identifying the causes of your stress makes it easier to manage. Consider some of the most common causes of stress. Do any of this sound familiar to you?

Common causes of stress
- Stress at work – maybe you're under pressure at work. Or you have recently become unemployed or retired.

- Family stress – maybe you're experiencing relationship problems at the moment. You might be going through a breakup or having an affair.

- Financial stress – suddenly you have huge bills to pay, and you need to borrow money. There's just not enough money for the month and so on.

- Health problems – maybe you were recently diagnosed with an illness, suffered an injury or lost someone you love.

- Stress from life in general - various life events from buying a dress for a wedding to planning for a holiday can all lead to feelings of stress.

Physical symptoms of stress include
- Headaches and or dizziness

- Muscle pain and or tension

- Stomach issues

- Chest pains and or a faster heartbeat

- Sexual issues

Mental symptoms of stress include
- Find it difficult to concentrate

- Find it difficult to make decisions

- Often overwhelmed

- Worrying too much

- Forgetful

How stress can cause changes in behavior

- Irritable and moody

- Not enough or too much sleep

- Not eating enough or eating too much

- Avoidance of people or certain places

- Drinking, drugs or smoking

The Two Types of Stress

The National Institute of Mental Health (NIMH) recognizes that there are two types of stress. Those are, acute stress and chronic stress.

Acute stress

Acute stress is the most common type of stress. People who are faced with pressure from recent events or upcoming challenges in the near future are likely to experience this type of stress. For example, maybe you were stressed out about a recent disagreement, or you have an upcoming deadline. Since the solutions tend to be clear and immediate acute stress is usually easier to overcome. Even with the most difficult of challenges there is often a clear way out.

Fortunately, because acute stress is short term it does not create any long-term side effects. Usually, you will be faced with short term side effects such as headaches, muscle tension, stomachache, or general distress. However, if acute stress is repetitive, it can become a long-standing problem and you should seek professional medical advice.

Chronic stress

Chronic stress develops over longer time periods and can be much more harmful to us. Causes are usually life circumstances such as a dysfunctional family, relationship problems, ongoing poverty or various other stresses. Additionally, early life traumatic experiences can also cause chronic stress. Chronic stress can contribute to cardiovascular, immune, sleep, respiratory and reproductive problems.

When a person is in a constant state of chronic stress it can lead to serious health problems such as diabetes, high blood pressure and heart problems. Mentally it can cause depression, post-traumatic stress disorder (PTSD), and many more real issues. If it continues unnoticed people are left feeling hopeless. Inevitably this could lead to a breakdown which may result in violence or even suicide. Again, if you suffer from any of these issues, please seek professional help.

The NIMH have concluded that there are three clear causes of stress:

Routine stress

This occurs from daily activities such as taking care of children, homework or finances and so on.

Sudden, disruptive changes

This occurs when there is a sudden change from normal life. That could be something like a job loss or a family bereavement.

Traumatic stress

This occurs as a result of extreme trauma such as an accident, assault, war, disaster and so on.

Anxiety

Anxiety is a normal emotion. According to The American Psychological Association (APA) it is.

"An emotion characterized by feelings of tension, worried thoughts and physical changes like increased blood pressure."

We all experience anxiety on some level. It only becomes a problem when people experience excessive levels of anxiety. On a mild level it can cause some unsettling feelings. Whilst at more severe levels it can greatly affect daily life leading to excessive fears, worry and nervousness. Worst case scenario it could develop into a health problem or a serious medical disorder. Such disorders affect behavior and emotions. Understanding the differences between normal anxiety and General Anxiety Disorder (GAD) which requires medical attention can help people to overcome their conditions.

When faced with potentially harmful or worrying situations it is normal for humans to feel anxious. In fact, it is necessary for survival. Since the beginning of human evolution predators have approached humans and set off alarms in their biology. Dangerous situations create an adrenaline rush of hormones from the brains which triggers anxiety. These cause noticeable effects such as a faster heartbeat, sweating and alertness. This is otherwise known as the "fight-or-flight' response, and it serves to protect humans from potential threats.

Of course, nowadays that isn't much use because we are no longer being chased by large predators. However, events in daily life still create this response. This is usually an overreaction that sends us into anxiety. Sure, in some situations such as dangerous ones it is a vital signal. But it is mostly unnecessary and not serving our benefit. Rather it is clouding our judgement and hurting our life.

Anxiety disorders

In extreme cases anxious feelings are out of proportion to the trigger cause or event. This is when anxiety goes further into becoming General Anxiety Disorder (GAD). Over reactions can cause physical symptoms including high blood pressure and nausea. The APA describes GAD as; *"Having recurring intrusive thoughts or concerns." When anxiety becomes a disorder, it begins to negatively impact daily life.*

Nearly forty million people are affected by GAD in the United States alone. In fact, it is one of the most common mental illnesses. Unfortunately, GAD doesn't have any instant solution. However, it can be effectively managed and less problematic through the use of specific tools and therapy. Symptoms of GAD include.

- Constant restlessness

- Unable to control feelings of worry

- Easily irritable

- Find it difficult to concentrate

- Problems with sleep

- Sleep difficulties

- Disruption of daily life

Depression and Rumination

Almost ten percent of the U.S adult population have at least one time experienced a significant bout of depression within the last year. People from all ages, races, ethnicities and socioeconomic backgrounds can experience depression. Some are lucky and will maybe only experience one depressive experience during their lifetime. But for many it can last much longer. Beyond feeling sad or going through a rough patch, those with depressive disorders have a serious mental health condition. Without treatment it can wreak havoc on their lives. Fortunately, with professional medication and treatment they can become better.

Overthinkers are often left feeling depressed. It can feel like a never-ending cycle of negative thoughts. This can cause lower energy levels and make them withdraw from social life. Simple daily activities can become overwhelming. On a biological level depression takes over the prefrontal cortex which is the logical thinking part of our brain. As a result of this hijack the brain is left feeling negative and hopeless. Indeed, we all have negative thoughts now and then. It's completely normal to feel sad or down sometimes. That's just how life can go. The problem is that these negative thoughts can start to continually replay in our minds. This is known as rumination, and it is a danger to our mental health. The more it prolongs the more it can intensify depression and our ability to think clearly.

Depression Symptoms

There are a number of different symptoms of depression

which depend on the individual. Usually, it changes each day, and a depressive episode lasts up to two weeks for the average person. Some common symptoms include.

- Insomnia

- Difficulty to concentrate

- Lower energy and less activity

- Lacking interest in activities

- Feelings of hopelessness

- Sleep inconsistency

- Appetite inconsistency

- Low interest in activities

- Hopelessness, suicidal or guilty thoughts

Causes of depression

There is no one single cause for depression. It can come about because of a number of reasons. Anything from a life crisis, physical illness or other stresses that occur in your life can contribute to depressive episodes. Consider some of these other common causes of depression.

Trauma

Some other causes of depression to take into account are traumas. People who have experienced a trauma when they were younger can be left with changes in their brains which might lead to depression. The same can be said for genetics. Some disorders tend to run in the family.

Life circumstances

Changes in life circumstances can influence a person developing depression. Some of those might be romantic status, changes in career, financial issues and general life changes. Or even where a person lives or works.

Medical conditions

People who have chronic illnesses and ongoing pains are more likely to experience depression. Some medications may also cause depression as a side effect. Consider what you put into your body.

Drug and alcohol misuse

Nearly a quarter of adults with substance abuse issues are reported to have experienced major depressive episodes. Usually, they are abusing drugs or alcohol to escape their depression and overthinking. But it's a trap of cycling into something much worse. Treatment for both problems is the solution. Again, consider what you put into your body.

Information Overload and Decision Making

Consider all of the information that comes your way on a daily basis. In today's modern digital world there is an avalanche of information coming at us every moment. Too much of it will overwhelm you. Add to this that when you have been living in the same place for a while it's natural to accumulate a lot of stuff. The same holds true in the digital domain. We store an excess of stuff that clogs up our laptops, phones and devices. Most of this stuff is unnecessary and it clouds our thinking. We are filling our lives with stuff that we really don't need. All of that fills up space in your mind too. Mental freedom is compromised, and it sucks your productivity and clouds your thinking.

For many of us this is a paradox. On one hand it is great having all of this choice. Whilst on the other hand it is disrupting our lives. It causes us to procrastinate simple decisions and be overwhelmed with all of the choices. The present world we are living in right now is a place of abundance. Masters of our realms we can curate the finest details of our lives. From what we eat to what we watch on the TV. Just imagine fifty years ago. You had to watch what was on TV at that moment. Whilst choices of what to eat or who to date were much more limited. Clearly, we are in a much better place nowadays. However, research has shown that having more choices can increase anxiety, paralysis and dissatisfaction. This is known as the paradox of choice. The author Barry Schwartz observed that having more options to choose from doesn't necessarily make people happier but it can cause them stress and make decisions difficult. Try focusing on an excess of life experience instead and live with a minimalist attitude towards materialism. More on this later in the chapter.

Insomnia

Picture this familiar scene. It's already past bedtime. You're in bed ready to sleep but you're still wide awake. Your mind races and thinks, "I have just eight hours to sleep before work". You check your phone and one hour has passed. The phone light fills the room. Still, you haven't slept a wink. Thoughts start to crowd your mind. Round and round the thoughts go and make you more tired but unable to sleep because your mind just won't switch off. The mistake many of us might make in this situation is to medicate. As you will find out later on, in most cases it is better to ride the dragon in a natural way than to lock it in a cupboard using medicine. We will explore natural remedies with far superior long-term benefits.

Negativity Bias

For over six hundred million years the human nervous system has been evolving. Yet it is still responding in the same ways to life threatening survival situations. In order to keep us safe and alive the human brain evolved to overestimate threats whilst underestimating opportunities and resources. This is known as the negativity bias which essentially is the human tendency to react more intensely to negative stimulus than positive.

When it comes to our thinking this translates to a default of overthinking and worrying more than is necessary. Threats and challenges are seen as much more than they really are. But we are no longer a primitive species living in caves. The modern world is a relatively much safer place.

The more we perceive something to be out of our control the more it can worry us. We try to think up every way to gain control. This is a difficult pattern to escape from. Many people don't want to have to suffer the shame of being a failure. So, they get stuck thinking of how not to fail. Catastrophes are imagined. The worst-case scenarios are thought up in detail. Inevitably the thoughts spiral faster and faster out of control.

Mental Health Conditions

There are numerous reasons for overthinking. Of course, these differ for each individual. As we explored many come from life situations and damaged thinking. Then there are some which are caused by health conditions. Mainly those include obsessive-compulsive disorder (OCD) and General Anxiety Disorder (GAD). Depression is another mental illness that causes negative thinking. See the earlier section for more information on that. Also, I will present solutions to that later on.

Obsessive-Compulsive Disorder (OCD)

OCD is a condition where a person experiences recurring thoughts or frequent behaviors that they cannot control. If you experience symptoms whereby, you're having unpleasant thoughts or negative behaviors then consider talking with a therapist. Additionally, there are some medicines that may help with more severe symptoms of OCD.

General Anxiety Disorder (GAD)

GAD is a condition where a person feels anxious most of the time. If you experience symptoms such as constant worry, a sense of dread or trouble concentrating then you may require treatment or medicine.

Cortisol

Additionally, when we are under stress the body releases the hormone called Cortisol. The right balance of this hormone is essential for our health. However, when we are under too much stress it makes our brain think we are in danger and so our cortisol levels become dangerously high. As a result, the body becomes weary and tired. At worst it can cause heart attacks, anxiety, depression and mental illness.

Again, if you suffer from any of these conditions, please contact a mental health professional for medical advice.

Now we have explored the causes of overthinking. This was an important step to take. As I mentioned, to effectively break free from overthinking you first need to understand the causes. Now with that in mind in the next chapter specific solutions to those causes will be presented.

ESCAPING
OVERTHINKING

In the previous chapter we looked at the main reasons for overthinking. Getting to the root of a problem is the best way to treat it. Now we can begin to come up with specific solutions to those specific causes. Let's explore.

How to manage stress

Managing stress effectively begins with recognizing when it is a problem. As I mentioned earlier some people use stress to fuel them. Think of that high powered executive burning off the fuels of stress to get through his hectic workday. That's not a great lifestyle. Eventually he will burn out or end up in a hospital. Plus, there is an alternative where you could be achieving much better results with much more fulfillment.

Remember you're not a superhero.

So, what's the solution? First of all, identify if you're experiencing any of the physical warning signs of stress. Do you suffer from tense muscles, headaches or tiredness? Identify any mental or behavioral warning signs of stress.

- Do you find it difficult to concentrate or make decisions?

- Are you often overwhelmed, forgetful or tend to worry too much?

- Do you find yourself too often be moody?

- Are you getting enough sleep or having too much?

- Are you eating right?

- Are you avoiding anyone or anything?

If you have identified any warning signs of stress, start to think about what is causing the stress. It could be coming from any of the areas I mentioned earlier.

Summary of common causes of stress
- Stress at work

- Family stress

- Financial stress

- Health problems

- Stress from life in general

Sort any issue into lists with practical solutions. Now that you have possible solutions out in front of you it's time to take small steps towards change. Make a plan to address whatever you can. Simple solutions could be cutting down on commitments, saying no or trying a new life change. Whatever it is, stick with it.

Review your lifestyle. You could well be taking on way too much. In that case it might be a good idea to delegate. Or you could just prioritize your life and focus more on what's important to you. Focus on cultivating supportive relationships. Spend time to cultivate and grow the relationships that really matter. Spend quality time with your friends and family. If you're lonely then expand your social life. Join some clubs, hobbies and activities. All these will have a positive impact on your life.

Finally build positive and healthy life habits. Make sure you are eating healthy. Plenty of nutrients and clean food. Workout consistently. Mix it up with cardio and weights. If you hate working out, join a sports club or a fitness class. There are so many ways to get fit. No excuses. If you smoke, drink or take drugs try to cut it out or stop it entirely. Give yourself some nice well-earned breaks now and then. Go for a walk-in nature. Or when you get really burned out take a nice long beach holiday. Get some quality sleep in by having a consistent bedtime and a consistent wake up time.

If you still struggle with stress, then consider getting professional help. That doesn't mean you're a failure. Your health is paramount, and professionals can give you a lift up. With their expertise they will be able to advise and treat you further.

How to manage anxiety

A life with anxiety can be troublesome. However, don't worry because there are clear steps that can help you to manage it. First of all, realize that anxiety has less strength when you focus your attention to the present moment. Clear your mind. When your anxiety levels rise, start to get back control by taking some deep breaths. This can restore harmony and center you back into the present moment. Try this simple exercise out. Follow the steps below.

- Sit in a comfortable position. Or lean against a wall.

- Close your eyes. Now begin to slowly breathe in through your nostrils. Follow this with a long breath out through your mouth.

- Try using a mantra as you are breathing in and out. It could be "present". Or "now". Whatever you prefer. Say it out loud as you breathe out.

- Keep practicing this powerful breathing exercise to make you stronger at fighting anxiety and staying present.

*For a more detailed version of this you can check out the meditation and mindfulness chapter.

Get to the root of your problem

Anxiety presents physical symptoms which can be overwhelming. Your heart beats out of control, you tremble and feel pain. Overwhelming, a big distraction that catches up your attention and cycles into a worse situation.

Discovering a solution requires getting to the root of what is causing the anxiety. Make some time to explore your feelings and thoughts. Using a journal to write your feelings can be a powerful tool for exploring the causes of your anxiety. Keep it beside your bed or in your work bag so that you can have easy access to it. Cultivate the habit of exploring the causes of your anxiety. In time you will work on solutions to the root cause. Yes, that will be much more powerful than dealing with the symptoms.

Each of us has our own triggers for anxiety. They can sometimes be obvious things such as too much caffeine, alcohol or smoking. Then sometimes it could be less obvious. Maybe it comes from financial or relationship situations. However, if you can identify the trigger then you can limit your exposure and response to it. Below are some of the most common triggers.

- Work related stress

- Relationships

- Genetics

- Withdrawal from medication or drugs

- Side effects of medication or drugs

- Driving or traveling

- Trauma

- Phobias such as fear of crowds or heights

- Chronic illnesses or pain

- Caffeine

Focus on solutions

Anxiety is often the result of fears from events that have never happened or are unlikely to happen. As an example, we worry that our job will be lost or that we might become ill. Indeed, life presents us with surprises and bad things often happen. You can't control that. Instead of focusing on what you can't control, focus on solutions. A powerful solution is to let go of that fear and focus on what you're grateful for. When bad things do actually happen instead of being imagined you also have the choice of how you respond to them. This is bringing the power back to you and away from the grip of anxiety. With practice you will effectively change your attitude and become more empowered.

"Between stimulus and response there is a space. In that space is our power to choose our response. In our response lies our growth and our freedom.", Viktor Frankl

Maintain great health

Diet, supplements and exercise are the best remedy to a long-term solution of beating anxiety. So much research proves this. Again, a healthy body equals a healthy mind and vice versa. Eat a well-balanced and clean diet with lots of fresh fruit and vegetables. Have less processed food and more pure meats and so on. Exercise regularly and make sure it wears you out and works up a sweat. Try out some supplements. Omega 3 and zinc are two great ones for the brain.

Redirect your focus

Additionally, you can redirect your focus away from anxiety to a new focus. Go and meet your friends for example. Or get involved in some enjoyable hobbies and activities. Here are some more examples to redirect your focus. Remember they should make you feel good or leave a sense of fulfillment.

- Clean the house or organize your workplace
- Do something creative such as writing or playing music
- Go out walking
- Do some sports or exercise
- Meditate
- Enjoy listening to music

- Read an inspiring book

- Watch an inspiring movie

Aromatherapy and relaxation

Candles, scents and incense can be a really soothing relief to anxiety. Dim the lights and experience some aromatherapy. It will activate certain receptors in your brain to relax the anxiety. In addition, you can put on some calming music. Stretch out and practice some yoga poses. Combine them with breathing and focusing on the present moment. Or you could meditate with the candles and aroma. Try this for just fifteen minutes a day or more and you will begin to feel much better.

How to manage depression

Finding the energy to take care of yourself and overcome depression can feel like a hard mountain to climb. That's why depression often lasts so long. It's almost easier to stay depressed than fight the beast. However, it is possible to overcome and manage the condition. It won't be a magic pill or quick fix. Here's how to break through.

Push back

When you're depressed it's like a cloud of negative thoughts blocks your mind. Negative thoughts blur your vision. "I'm sick of this" "nothing ever goes my way" "How could I be so dumb". When you're in the whirlwind of those thoughts life can be unbearable. No wonder doing simple things becomes so hard. What you've got to do in those situations is to push back on those thoughts. Start questioning them and take a different point of view. Get up out of your chair and say no! Push back and come up with alternatives to those thoughts. It could be a rapid fire of attention. "I'm sick of this" becomes "I will beat this" or "I'm better than this" and so on. "Nothing ever goes my way" becomes "this won't last forever" or "soon the tides will turn my way, it's just a matter of time" and so on. You get the process. Now go ahead and push back.

Positive vibes

Depression episodes often bring back painful memories. Falling down that black hole of negative thoughts the depressed person is drawn further and further into the darkness. The dark feelings overwhelm them and the deeper they fall. But it doesn't need to be that way. Break free and pull yourself up. Force yourself to focus on a more positive memory. Think back on your life. What was your happiest memory? When did you feel happy recently? Go back to that memory. Visualize it. See what you saw, hear what you heard and feel what you felt. Take a moment or as long as you want to go deep into those happy memories. Anytime the darkness falls on you go back and visit those happy memories again. That will put a smile on your face.

Keep smiling. When people ask you how you're doing, tell them you're doing great. I know you're probably not and you prefer to be down but push back on that. Tell them something good. Take care of yourself. People with depression often neglect their health and basic hygiene. Make sure you keep up with showers, brushing teeth and practice good hygiene. In addition, eat a healthy diet and stick with regular exercise.

Make Plans

When you're feeling depressed, your energy will be low. Tucked up under the bed covers feels like the best place to be. It's become easier and easier to live this way. Almost everything can be delivered right to your home so there isn't much need to go out or to make plans. But to overcome depression it's essential that you make an effort to make plans and fill your days. Get up in the morning, take a shower and get out there. Fill your days up. It will give you something to look forward to. Even scheduling a walk or mediation in there will give you more purpose and shift you away from depressive episodes.

Stay connected and find support

Social connection is directly related to inner wellbeing and mental health. Problem with depression is that it causes us to withdraw. Much like pushing back on depression you need to stay connected socially. Confide in your friends and family. If they are not around schedule in a call with them. Even better if you can go meet them in real life. If you have a smaller social circle, then join some online groups and forums. Step out of your comfort zone and join some meetups, sports clubs or even try volunteering. The chamber of commerce, toastmasters and dance classes are all very good general places to get connected with others.

Remember that depression doesn't have to define you. It is a common mental illness and one that can be treated. Remember to reach out for support and to take excellent care of your health. You're worth it.

How to manage information overload

Do you struggle to focus? Maybe your to-do list doesn't ever stop growing and it always feels like you're getting nowhere. Each day is a struggle in a cluttered world. Excessive mental clutter affects every area of your life. From how long it takes you to do things to how much pleasure you gain from life. It can distract you, weigh you down and bring chaos into your life. Faced with an avalanche of clutter, people freeze up and just don't know where or how to get started. Procrastination, doubt and overthinking clouds their minds. Oh, there's always something more important or more interesting to be doing. Oh, how about that new series on Netflix. Or how about the new YouTube podcast or calling your friend. All of these can be welcome distractions. Practiced in moderation they are fine. As long as you get done what you need to get done.

A mountain is climbed one step at a time and an avalanche begins with one snowflake. Both consist of many parts and steps. The same is true when it comes to decluttering your mind. With a little bit of time each and every day you can begin to gain an advantage over the clutter. Start to reap the rewards of a clutter free life. From reduced stress to more productivity and much, much more. The combination of small parts and steps build up to big efforts in the long run. Here's how.

Eliminate the nonessential and do more of what you love

The first step to dealing with information overload is to start reducing your commitments. Realize that the busier you become the more your life becomes cluttered. When you're feeling this way, take a look at the different areas of your life. Write out all the commitments that you currently have (this will be an eye-opening experience). Ask yourself.

- Does it bring you joy?

- Does it add value?

- Is it worth your time?

These questions will help you to decide whether to continue with each commitment or to reduce how much time you spend on it or to drop it all together. Get comfortable with being able to say no and to politely decline opportunities. Make sure those are the right things for you or not. Be graceful. Eliminating the things that have less meaning to you will open up the door to doing more of what you love. In perspective from this point of view you can analyze each commitment and decide if it is bringing positivity to your life.

Plan your days

Take a look at your day-to-day life. We all have our own set ways and habits. But without structure our days can end up in chaos. Make a plan for your days. This is best done the evening before or first in the morning. Having that structure might seem like it's limiting you, but it is actually freeing you because it keeps the mind from wandering off into negative thought patterns. It's a great exercise to write out your weekly and daily plans, appointments and routines. Have this written where you can see it and try to stick with it. Bring calmer and rationality to your life. No more being at the whim of negative influences and getting caught up doing meaningless things which will cause negative emotions such as guilt or shame later on.

Spend most of your time with positive people

This is going to sound cruel, but you need to potentially stop seeing certain people in your life. Some friendships simply clutter your life. Instead, spend most of your time with positive people who make you happy and encourage you to grow. Sure, some of those toxic friendships might be fun because you hang out, play video games and drink beers. A little bit of vice is fine but too much of it and it's not advancing your life. Therefore, you need to move on. Maybe you need to get out there and make new friendships that are more positive. Consider taking up some hobbies, sports or solo traveling. All of these will put you into direct contact with ambitious and outgoing people. Those will result in positive and mutually beneficial friendships.

Become more organized

Clearing up the physical spaces you work and live in is an excellent exercise to increase productivity and reduce mental fog. Head to your office. Begin by clearing off your desk. Take literally everything off it and either store it or throw it out. Additionally give it a nice clean wipe down. Follow the same process for your living area. Clean out the piles of things, then wipe it down or brush it up. In fact, you should be doing this weekly or even daily. Follow Jordan Peterson's advice and "tidy your room". Mind over clutter.

Taking things, a step further it's a great idea to become even more organized and systematic. Try setting up an alphabetical filing system for each of your projects. The same can be done online with tools such as Trello and Monday.com. It's useful to label things and prioritize them. Schedule out your appointments using a calendar. Whilst you're on the computer get rid of any files or programs that you don't use. Clean up your emails, bookmarks and data. Reduce the number of subscriptions you have. Install some blocking software for websites that distract you. Make sure you do all of this regularly otherwise that clutter will once again build up and stress you out.

Remove any distractions

A famous study from the University of San Diego found that whenever you're distracted it triggers the fight or flight response in your brain. So, each time there is a new notification on one of your devices it causes your train of thought to get lost. Start making an effort to remove any distractions that take away your focus. Close all browser tabs except the one you're working on. Uninstall applications during your work hours. Put your phone on silent. Turn off all notifications on any of your devices and put your phone away.

Naturally we will need a break after periods of working. But you should not just dive into a social media feed. That will just overload your mind. Instead try taking a short walk, listen to a soothing song or wander around your room. Set boundaries. When you become consistent with the processes of decluttering, you're going to find you're feeling less stressed and happier. Remember to begin small and stick with it daily.

Minimalism

Minimalism is a practice that can help you to become freer from overthinking and overload. In essence it is a tool to eliminate excess so that you can focus on what is important. As a result, you will be living closer to fulfillment, happiness and freedom. A few of the other benefits include more time for your passions, living in the moment, more creativity, better health, peace of mind and much more.

Now there is nothing wrong with owning some material possessions. That is completely normal. The problem is when it becomes out of control and just unnecessary. Fact is today's society owns too much stuff and gives too much meaning. We put owning that dream car or house above our health. We are willing to overwork ourselves in the pursuit of owning material possessions at the detriment of our health. We buy clothes to fit in with the crowd and align with the current fashion trends. But most material things don't give us lasting, deep happiness or fulfilment. The feeling it gives us is fleeting. Sure, some of these things might be important to you. Having a basic level of comfort and confidence is awesome. Materialism is very useful for that.

The concept of minimalism will allow you to decide if certain material possessions are good for you or not. In turn it can help you to pursue a more purpose driven life. Nowadays that is more important than ever. There is an excess in the world, way too much noise and way too little meaning. Minimalism can help in getting rid of the non-essential so that you can focus on what really matters.

There is a common misconception about minimalism that it means to live like a monk with no possessions. No, to me that just sounds boring and sterile. Minimalism doesn't need to be like that at all. Basically, it's about clearing away the non-essential and unnecessary. Which in turn gives you more room for what you truly want plus more peace and time. You can take this as far as you want. From simply getting rid of a few things to living a basic, simple life.

So how do you get started with minimalist living? Begin with giving your house, room or apartment a good clean out. Get rid of all the clutter. Throw things out you no longer use. Those clothes you didn't wear for more than three months would be better off at a donation center instead of gathering dust in your wardrobe. Tidy up your desk. Tidy up your computer. Cut down your unnecessary appointments and identify where you are wasting time. You'll find all of this will leave you much lighter mentally. There are no set rules or one particular way to live minimally. In general, it is to simplify living without unnecessary possessions and distractions.

How to make better decisions

Every day we are presented with endless decisions to make.

From what food to eat to bigger decisions such as who to marry or what company to work for. On and on the list goes. Because of so many choices and overthinking, many of us struggle with making decisions. We feel it's normal to think about decisions. But at what point does it become irrational to overthink decisions? Well of course that depends on the context. Indeed, some decisions do require more thought. But it should always be a deliberate and active thought. Overthinking small decisions will just lead us astray.

The answer is to get comfortable making decisions. Sometimes our decisions might not work out how we want to. We have to learn to be ok with accepting and standing by our decisions whatever the outcome. In addition, reduce the number of decisions you need to make. Take a leaf out of Steve Jobs' book who wore the same style of clothing every day. Or Barack Obama who wears only gray or blue suits. Such habits will help break you free from decision fatigue and give you more power to focus on the important things. Here are some more ways to overcome overthinking when making decisions.

Set a time limit on your decisions
Never rush yourself but put a limit on the amount of time to make a decision. This will make you more effective and also improve your time management skills. Some big decisions you

might want to sleep on or come back to later on so you can see if the situation has changed. Other decisions you shouldn't spend more than a few minutes on. Learn to prioritize and allocate the right amount of time for each decision.

Give yourself time to think

When presented with an important decision most people rarely give themself a chance to sit there with the decisions. Instead, they fill their mind with other stuff such as scrolling social media or busying themselves with nonsense. Then they arrive at a bad decision. Not a smart way. Set aside time and be in the moment with just you and your mind to think on that decision. This is essential for big decisions. Use writing paper or a document to help you record your thoughts. Or go take a walk and reflect on it. Being in the present moment with the decisions will allow you to focus on what matters right now and to in turn make better decisions.

Use a decision model

There are some great models for making decisions out there. One method I recommend is to set up the options for a decision and then weight the value of each option. The scores of each option can then be tallied to present a clear winner. However, remember this will utilize cold logic. Take into account your gut and heart emotions. Again, it is useful to be in the present moment or to limit the time when making the decision.

How to manage Insomnia

Instead of taking sleeping pills which often become addictive there are some natural ways to overcome insomnia overthinking. First of all, try to stick to a regular time to go to bed and wake up. A window of seven to nine hours is optimal. So, for example I go to bed at midnight and wake up at 8am. Choose times that work for you and try to get as close to those times as possible. If you miss those windows, then you essentially missed a sleep cycle. A sleep cycle is around ninety minutes so just be aware of that. It could be another ninety minutes or more before the next window. Before you sleep try to wind down your screen time on devices. Around an hour before bedtime, let your mind relax. Try to meditate or journal so that your mind is more settled. Still if you can't sleep, don't try to fight it. Resist the urge to stimulate your mind with watching TV or looking at your phone. Try something more calming such as reading a book or listening to relaxing music. Avoid taking sleeping pills unless prescribed. People who take sleeping pills tend to build a tolerance to them. They end up relying on them and need them more and more. Better to stay natural.

How to manage medical conditions

If you have tried all of the above solutions in this chapter and none have helped you then maybe, it's time to seek medical help. There are so many options. You could see a therapist or mental health professional who can get to the roots of your problem and help you to make a plan to overcome them. Why suffer more? Working with a counselor, therapist or medical professional will help you gain insights and find solutions. That could be therapy, medicine or more. Reach out to your health care provider before it's too late.

Now we have discovered some solutions to common causes of overthinking. It's now time to take a look at how we can deal with negative thoughts.

FREEDOM FROM NEGATIVE THOUGHTS & THE NEGATIVE BIAS

Imagine you're at a restaurant and the waiter gives you a mean look. How would you feel? Would you take it personally? Or would you think, "Oh maybe this guy is just having a bad day." Or are you the kind of person to take it personally and think something like "it must be because of me; I look so terrible today". Beware because those small things you take personally start to build up and it can disturb you for sustained periods of time. Negative thoughts linger.

According to leading psychologist and author Martin Seligman there are three primary causes of negative thoughts.

Fear of the Future

It's common for people to fear the unknown. In a future that has not yet happened it can be easy to imagine the worst-case scenarios. Panic and worry are the result.

Anxiety About the Present

Typically, people with low self-esteem and confidence worry what others think of them. Or they worry about whether they are doing a good job or not. Anxiety is the result.

Past regret

All of us have once done something we feel ashamed or embarrassed about. We are humans and none of us are perfect. Depression and shame are the result.

Negative thoughts can feel so real. They make us feel upset, anxious and worried. Life is no longer fun, and the joy has been taken out. Like a bad taste it sticks in your mouth. It can even go as far as affecting your health. All that negative thinking leaves you sick and tired. No one wants this. So how do we deal with negative thoughts?

First and foremost, realize that you do not have to accept them as reality. Next work on replacing your negative thoughts with thoughts that are more positive and that make you feel better. Think about it differently. For example, if you're going through a tough time. You might think "I wish my life was like the good old days". Instead, you could think about it like this. "This is a challenge now, but I will get through it and my life will be better than ever before." This isn't about lying to yourself. All of what was said is true. Simply put you reframed it to be more motivating. Now that is a much more powerful way of thinking.

Are there any negative thoughts troubling you right now? Listen to your thoughts. Don't run away from them. Discover yourself. Maybe you find that you're being too hard on yourself or are having unnecessary negative thoughts. Come up with something more encouraging. After all you're the one who is in charge of your thoughts so get in the driver seat and take control.

Yes, and also take this seriously. Don't make the mistake of thinking these are just thoughts and that they are no big deal. Absolutely not. There is a strong connection between the mind and the body. Thoughts can directly affect your health. Positive thoughts cause your brain to release chemicals that can make your immune system stronger, lower blood pressure and improve overall health. As a direct result it makes you stronger and more resistant to illness. Plus, you will feel much happier about your life. Let's take a look at some more solutions.

Simple ways to deal with negative thoughts

Acceptance and Commitment Therapy (ACT)

ACT is a method of reconfiguring your relationship to your thoughts. It works by defusing overthinking through exploring thoughts to gain control on them. Instead of trying to eliminate negative thinking ACT focuses on trying to change how we react to thoughts. The majority of human thought is random and can often be destructive. Thinking is a never-ending mental stream; millions of thoughts are happening all the time and we are not fully able to control what thoughts arise. At best only five percent is meaningful and relevant. But we can control how we respond to them. Forming a new relationship with our thoughts can free us from the paralysis of negative thoughts.

Incidentally this way of reframing our thoughts has been around for a very long time. Buddhism and modern psychology were built on many of these concepts. You can find this practiced in mindfulness and cognitive therapy. Buddhist meditation instructs the student to become aware of their thoughts and observe them as consciousness. To not take them personally or push them away is a founding precept of the mediation practice.

The Buddha divided thoughts into two categories. There are wholesome thoughts which lead to peace and happiness. Then there are negative thoughts which lead to harm and stress. The mind dwells on its particular tendencies. If you're more sensitive to negative thinking, then your mind will be more likely to end up in a negative state. But if you train your mind, it can become more positive. To experience more happiness and inner peace work on becoming more observant and in control of your thinking.

Start to become open and curious to your thoughts as they arise. You don't need to believe in your thoughts or take action on them. Instead explore them with curiosity. Just like a psychologist would suggest you do. First notice your thoughts and investigate them. Especially any negative thoughts. Reflect on them and it will help to break their power.

Let's take a look at some examples of dealing with negative

thought patterns. Imagine that you were just diagnosed with a serious illness. Maybe you tell yourself

"My life will never be the same" or "that's it for me".

Anything thinking like that is going to make you feel much worse than you already do. Why not work on becoming better? It begins in the mind. Try to reframe your thoughts to something like;

"Well, this won't last forever, I will get better than before".

Don't hurt yourself twice. There are millions of stories out there of people overcoming the odds. Get inspired by them.

In addition to ACT, I will offer you some more simple techniques to deal with negative thoughts. Realize that eliminating negative thoughts forever is unrealistic. As I mentioned it's human to feel sad or down sometimes. After all, it makes the highs in life that much better. Now a more realistic and sustainable way to manage negative things is to gain control of them. Changes won't happen overnight. It will require practice and commitment on a daily basis.

Challenge your negative thoughts

When a persistently negative thought arises, question it. Ask yourself at least five questions. You can use these examples and tailor them to suit you. Have them stored on your phone or somewhere with quick easy access. Even better if you can memorize them. Consider the following.

- Is this a true thought?

- Is this thought serving me or hurting me?

- Can I turn it into something positive or can I learn from it?

- What would my life be like without this thought?

- Is this thought hiding the truth from me about something that I am avoiding?

Focus on your feelings right now

Say that you feel sad at the moment. Focus on that sadness. But realize that the sadness isn't going to last forever. You're not doomed to feel this sadness forever. How long it lasts depends on how long you let it stay with you or when you decide to let it go.

When you find yourself in a state of overthinking take a moment to question whether your thoughts are coming from negativity or lack. Or are they coming from a more powerful place? Notice the thoughts of negativity creep up and start to spiral out of control as they gather speed. Recognize the patterns. The difference is that from negativity or lack the overthinking is not serving you. On the other hand, if it comes from power then this is beneficial to you. The better you become at recognizing the patterns the easier it will become to tune into a more productive state of mind. Learn to recognize when your overthinking starts.

Socialize

All of us experience negative thoughts. Realize you're not the only one.

Confide in someone you trust. Share your feelings with them and open up. The more open, the more you gain. Good friends will comfort you and help you to gain new perspectives. Take time to enjoy life with your family and friends. We are social animals, and it is in our nature to connect with others. It's well known that the people you spend the most time with end up influencing you the most. They will contribute to your habits and life choices. Spend most of your time with people you aspire to be like. If someone is a bad influence on you, have the courage to step away from them. Take time to grow a great social life. Join clubs, hobbies and get out there in the world. Socializing will also get you out of your head. Additionally, it will give you a larger support network.

You're not in this alone. It doesn't have to be that way. Look at the most successful people. Behind every successful person you will usually find countless mentors, support, friends and family who helped them get there. Even the tough Navy Seals have a team to back them up. You might think they got there alone but they were all helped.

'It is not true that I am self-made. Like everyone, to get to where I am, I stood on the shoulders of giants. My life was built on a foundation of parents, coaches, and teachers; of kind souls,' Arnold Schwarzenegger

'I get my knack for relationships from my mother,' Arianna Huffington

Find your support group and mentors. There are so many

benefits. From overcoming your strengths to identifying your weaknesses and working towards success. Sometimes it can be something as simple as having a shoulder to cry on. Even if you think you're strong, fearless and can go it all alone it helps to have some support. Maintaining a positive mindset all the time is practically impossible. There will be times you feel weak and want to quit. With a support group they will help to push you back up.

Support groups and mentors are great. Sometimes we need the kick to fire us into action. Accountability is awesome for that. Maybe you have been slacking off. Your accountability group or partner will be responsible for getting you back on track. It's their duty to ensure you stick to your words and commitments. Find people with similar goals and visions. Agree to push each other along.

Health and Fun

The simple science of eating well, sleeping well and exercising has a direct effect on your mindset. As mentioned earlier the mind and body are closely connected. Therefore, if you have a healthy body your mind will be healthy and vice versa. Join a gym and start a workout program. Or take up some sports. Go for walks. Once you're exercising right, remember to eat right. Consume the optimum number of calories and nutrients for your goals. Don't go over or under. Make sure you eat plenty of fresh fruits and vegetables. Take vitamins, live long and be healthy. Many of us are our own worst enemies at times. Guilt or desire and shame make us work too hard and feel bad about ourselves. Rarely do we take time to reward ourselves, to sit back, enjoy life and play. Find something that makes you laugh. Have fun and enjoy life. Again and again, I recommend great health because it is so super important!

Distraction

Distraction is a great remedy to overthinking. Have some hobbies that you can easily get involved in when you find yourself stuck in periods of overthinking. Maybe you play chess, cards or video games. It could even be getting up to stretch. Visualization is one of the most helpful and easy to implement distractions to negative thinking which you can use at anytime and anyplace. When that negative thought arises, close your eyes and picture yourself doing something you love. That could be playing music, sports, partying with friends or making love and so on. Go through the images in detail and play them out in your mind. Give yourself at least thirty seconds to visualize that experience. Feel the feelings, see the images and hear the sounds. Make it a vivid experience. Over time your brain will become accustomed to switching from a negative to a positive situation.

Writing

Writing out your negative thoughts is a great way to throw them out of your mind. This will clear your head. You can use a pen and paper or even a laptop or phone notes. Remember that writing with pen and paper is proven to be more effective but on digital format is fine also. Depends on how bad your handwriting is or if you want to store it. Personally, I like to store the notes and reflect on my progress years later. Whereas some like to write on paper and then burn it! What a great way to be released from your thoughts. Go crazy and write out all the bad stuff and be as honest with yourself as possible. No tricks or lies. Be truthful and make the most of it.

When you realize that negative thoughts are part of the mind and that you're not responsible for them it will help to break free from any attachment to them. The more we practice, shifting into our attention and thought patterns the more our mind begins to form strong and positive pathways. It takes time but it will be worth it in the long run.

A grateful mind cannot be a hateful mind. Positivity and negativity cannot occupy the same mind at the same time. Everyday there are millions of things to be grateful for.

Become aware of them. Write them down. Think about them.

At this point we can realize how helpless negative thinking patterns can leave us feeling. Put an end to the suffering. Practicing the right technique is the breakaway that will effectively retrain your negative thinking habits. Now let's work on breaking those patterns with one more powerful way of dealing with negative thinking.

Cognitive Restructuring

Thought modification otherwise known as cognitive restructuring is a powerful yet simple technique that has been proven to treat various mental health issues including depression and anxiety. It is helpful for identifying and changing negative thinking patterns. In fact, for anyone who struggles with negative thinking it can be a great remedy.

Thoughts and emotions happen automatically. Problem is when we are upset and in reaction then we are more likely to do stupid stuff that pacifies our feelings. For example, we take drugs, drink beer, eat junk food or waste time procrastinating and so on. All of that can spiral out of control. Cognitive restructuring helps us to notice our bad mental habits and replace them with more positive ones. When we use cognitive restructuring, it can help you to become more aware and in the moment. Simply put, it hands the power back to you. Instead of being something uncontrollable that just happens to you.

Think of the cognitive restructuring process as a way of organizing yourself mentally. Just like making a to-do list it helps you to be more organized and less overwhelmed. That's the premise of it all and that will allow you to have more brain power to focus on the important and bigger picture of your life. Negative thoughts are poison that comes with a corresponding negative emotion. If you can cut that out and reframe your thoughts, then you will be much better off.

When we can learn to be consistent with this process (which takes time by the way), it will create a positive impact on every area of your life. Whenever that challenge or conflict comes up you can be more flexible in how you react to it. This will change how you think and feel about everything. Here are just some of the real-world benefits of Cognitive Restructuring.

Become better at managing worry and anxiety
The mental habit of worry drives all anxiety issues. From

obsessive compulsive disorder (OCD) to social anxiety and general anxiety disorder (GAD). Worry is caused when we irrationally expect unrealistic threats or dangers in the future. Even though there is a part of us that knows logically that these worries are irrational it is still a habit that is very hard to break. Cognitive Restructuring can be used to effectively identify the times when we engage in patterns of worrying. It can then help to replace it with more realistic and helpful thought patterns.

Break free from rumination and depression

Rumination is the mental process of continually going over past mistakes and turning them over and over again in your mind. This is always in a negative way. Whilst worry is about the future, rumination concerns thinking about the past. Similar to worry, being a key driver for anxiety rumination is also a key driver. In this case it is a key driver for depression.

Rumination can be difficult to break this habit. Just like worrying, it is a strong thinking pattern, and it is addictive. People have become so used to it. Again, Cognitive Restructuring can help to break rumination. This works by first of all identifying the depression thought patterns and then replacing them with something more positive and empowering.

Stress relief

The human mind is able to think, critically, analyze and evaluate. Such a unique and great strength. However, without control it can also become a great weakness. For example, if we are analyzing a conversation we had whilst trying to sleep then it is not very helpful. Ultimately patterns of thinking like this can lead to stress and burnout. Cognitive Restructuring can improve our ability to switch from a thinking and critical mind to a more relaxed one at the suitable time. This is a great way to handle stress as it comes up.

Stop procrastinating and become more productive

Becoming distracted from time to time is completely normal. Even putting things off or on hold for a period of time is normal too. However, when we experience a wave of negative thinking about taking action is when it becomes problematic. Or when you never get anything done and those deadlines just pass you by. Maybe you have an endless list of tasks to do in your mind. Or maybe you're plagued by repeated criticism of yourself. The last thing anyone needs is a monkey on their back bothering them. That will just waste all of your energy.

Time passes us by. Most of that time is spent procrastinating.

When we are faced with a difficult challenge, we often waste tons of time avoiding it. We then tend to get busy with everything else but that. I know we are all guilty of that. Then we have the excuse that we are simply too busy. All these things we need to do again begin to pile up in our brain and constantly nag at us day and night. That is until you actually get them done or you delegate. Again, all of this avoiding, indecision and procrastination are contributing factors to overthinking and mental anguish. The best solutions to avoid those avoidance coping mechanisms at all costs. Of course, the best way is to just get on with it and do it. Right?

Cognitive Restructuring can effectively resolve procrastination problems. Through reprogramming our destructive thinking patterns, it helps us to take action and get things done. Take a deep breath and get it done. Be decisive and take action right now. Take action now and get done what you have been procrastinating. It might seem unpleasant but you're probably blowing things up and out of proposition in your mind. Once you get that done you will feel so much better with it behind you. Tackle things one by one and gain massive momentum.

Better communication and relationships
Communication is the key to building and maintaining

healthy relationships. We need to be able to express ourselves and listen with empathy. The same is true about how we talk to ourselves. If we constantly worry about offending others, then it will be difficult to assert ourselves and achieve what we want from a relationship. Or if we constantly judge and are hard on ourselves then we will have trouble getting anywhere in life. Cognitive Restructuring can help to improve the way we talk to ourselves. As a result, this will simultaneously improve our communication with others.

Increased Optimism

Sometimes it feels like there's just bad things going on everywhere in the world. But we don't need to have a pessimistic viewpoint. Sometimes you need to rise above it all and take the lead out. Cognitive Restructuring can help you to have a more optimistic view on life and a higher level of general happiness. Learning to examine and modify our habitual thinking patterns helps us to catch those overly negative or pessimistic thoughts. Many of those influences come from what is going on around you. Such as the news, media and so on. Turn those off and get in the control seat of your life.

Overcoming addiction

If you struggle with addictions, then I know you understand

how destructive your behaviors can be. Mindset and self-talk play a key role in the root cause of addictions and their associated behaviors. If your goal is to make progress and break free from your addictions, then Cognitive Restructuring can help you gain the mental mastery you will require to manage your cravings. When you gain control of your thoughts it extends into your behaviors which will in turn curb your addictive patterns. Simply it makes it easier to manage your thoughts and actions rather than them controlling you.

Increased confidence and assertiveness

Success in life depends on how well you can express the honest and true intentions of yourself in a respectful way. When we hold ourselves in high regard, we start to believe in who we are, and we pursue the goals we want. No matter how we feel on a given day we still persevere. Without confidence and assertiveness, we are left at the side to fight for the scraps and a life that we don't really want. This just gets worse. Use Cognitive Restructuring to build a more powerful inner voice and witness the effects create an increased confidence.

"I hated every minute of training, but I said, 'Don't quit. Suffer now and live the rest of your life as a champion.'" It isn't the mountains ahead to climb that wear you out; it's the pebble in your shoe.", Muhammad Ali

Cognitive Restructuring Steps

The fundamental principle of Cognitive Restructuring is based on cognitive mediation. This states that the way we feel in our emotions is not because of what has happened to us but rather it is the result of how we think about what has happened to us. For example, imagine you're at a party. You say hi to a stranger, but they ignore you. Do you take it personally and negative self-talk starts? Or maybe do you assume they are having a bad day or that they are just not on your vibe?

For the person who is more likely to take it personally and fall into a negative self-talk then you for sure you will benefit from Cognitive Restructuring. The process can be taken step by step. Together, let's take a look at those steps one by one.

Step 1, Stop and reflect

When you begin to feel a strong negative feeling instead of reacting to it, stop and reflect on it. Have an attitude of curiosity. We can use our earlier example of the stranger at the party.

- Begin by thinking of the emotions you felt and the thoughts you had.

- Ask yourself; What's going on here?

Step 2, Identify the trigger

What happened? You recognized a strong emotion inside of you. Your next step is to find out what triggered it. This could be something in the external environment such as a car cutting you off or in our example talking to a stranger who ignored you. It could even be an internal thought. To help identify the trigger;

Use; what, who, when, where questions?

- You talked to a stranger, and he ignored you

Step 3, Notice automatic thoughts

What were your first thoughts? Our first thoughts are on autopilot. They are our default thoughts and are pretty much out of our control. All of us have automatic thoughts and most of the time we don't recognize them. Cognitive Restructuring teaches us to become more aware of them and examine them closely. In our example;

- You felt rejected.

    - Why did he ignore me?

- Automatic thought

  - I must be a bad person because otherwise he would have been more friendly. Maybe I'm just a loser.

Step 4, Identify your emotion and its intensity

What were your first emotions? Mental interpretations of what happened create emotions. Each person's thinking causes different types and intensity of emotions. Say you have strong, angry reactions then of course you will be the type to get angry easily. Whereas if you experience thoughts of fear and worry then you will likely get anxious. In many cases you can get a mix of emotions often with one being more dominant.

- You felt sad and upset. Plus, some sadness.

  - Rate it on a scale from 1-10

Step 5, Come up with alternative thoughts

Are there any alternative ways that you could think about what happened? Now that you have identified your trigger, automatic thoughts and emotions you can now work on restructuring them. First, come up with alternatives to your automatic thoughts. If someone cut you off in traffic instead of being angry, be grateful that they didn't crash into you. Come up with as many alternatives as possible. Those should disengage from negative thought patterns but also be realistic. Gratitude is great for this. Let's look at our earlier example.

- Maybe that guy was having a bad day.

- Maybe you didn't talk loudly enough, and he didn't hear you.

- Maybe he is a bad guy and you're better off not knowing him anyway. Luckily, we didn't talk.

- Feeling grateful.

Step 6, Re-evaluate your emotional intensity

How do you feel now? Alternatives to your automatic thoughts should lower your emotional intensity. The more realistic and believable they are the more effective they will be at reducing emotional intensity. Challenging, questioning and then reframing your thoughts and feelings will certainly make you less upset. Plus, you're now in control.

Stick with the mental habit of Cognitive Restructuring. At first it will require a much more active approach. Commit to learning how to organize your thoughts and then modify them. The more you train your brain the stronger it gets at developing this new positive way of thinking. The rewards will make you want to stick with it as your negative feelings subside.

From now on whenever those negative thoughts come up, start the steps of cognitive restructuring or any of the previous techniques and tools. Try and test them all out. Then go with what works for you. That could change depending on the situation, your mood, causes and so on. Be flexible and adaptable. Now we have dealt with negativity. Now let's build up our armor in the next chapter. Let's take a look at its opposite, positivity and how it helps you deal with overthinking.

POSITIVITY

Positivity! Now I'm sure you've all heard that word before. But I guess it feels a little cheesy with all the self-help gurus out there burning that word out. By definition, the root meaning of positivity is to think in an optimistic way. A way that expects successful results and focuses on being happier. In essence it is a happy and worry-free state that focuses on the positives of life.

"Always look on the bright side of life", Monty Python

Is your glass half-empty or half-full? The answer to this will give you insights into your attitudes about yourself. It will help you to discover whether you're an optimistic or pessimistic person. Those very attitudes directly affect your health. Many studies have proven this. Optimism and positivity are essential to effectively managing stress. Naturally a less stressed-out person is more healthy because they have lower blood pressure, less cortisol and free radicals messing up their health.

An optimistic person is more resilient to the swings of life. They don't take things personally. Worrying about the future or regretting the past doesn't bother them much. Instead of being consumed by overthinking they are able to focus on achievement and actually doing the things they enjoy. Negative feelings are diminished and good feelings are the result. Positivity, love, joy, happiness and inspiration.

Don't get me wrong here. Being positive is not a state of ignorance. Maybe you've seen those people who at all costs try to avoid negative feelings. Like a forced smile, you can tell it's not authentic. Simply that's just burying your head in the sand and ignoring the challenges of life. Such thinking won't get you anywhere fast. True positivity does not try to avoid negative feelings. Instead, it is completely aware of them. Power and growth come in acknowledging them so that you can learn from them and work on becoming better. That will give you the courage to keep going when things get tough. Maybe you think that this is not for you. It seems so far off.

But don't worry it can be achieved. Training your mind to become more positive is a real thing.

Scientific research continues to research how positive thinking affects health. So far, they have found that it benefits some of the following.

- Longer life spans

- Reduced depression

- Lower stress levels

- Improved immunity

- Better physical health and well being

- Better heart health and less risk to cardiovascular disease

- Strong ability to endure stress and challenges

Positive thinking begins with correct self-talk

There is an endless stream of unspoken thoughts going on in everyone's heads all of the time. Those thoughts are automatic. They can be negative, or they can be positive. If they tend to be more negative, then you're likely to be more pessimistic. Whilst if your thoughts are mostly positive then you're more likely an optimist. In addition, positive and optimistic people usually live much healthier lifestyles. It's all a positive cycle of influence and all the habits stack up.

Life is an amazing and wonderful adventure. Instead of having a glass half full mentality we need to look on the bright side of life. Problem is that most of us tend to default being negative. That's something that evolution installed into us. Our brains began as lizards and our natural flight or fight behaviors remain. Anger triggers us to attack or panic. So, we tend to find ourselves still stuck in this thinking that we are going to be attacked by a predator. As much as we have advanced as humans, our biology still holds us back.

The human mind on a normal day can produce up to fifty thousand thoughts a day. Not surprisingly we can't control all of those thoughts. According to research almost seventy five percent of what we think is negative and works against us. To begin with, the odds are stacked against us! We know this from the previous chapter discussing the negativity bias. But just how can we possibly overcome this? What is required is a more deliberate and positive thinking.

Realize that positive thoughts aren't going to just appear in your mind. You need to actively take responsibility and engage in thinking positively. Remember how great you are and the amazing things you have achieved. Big yourself up and be grateful. This habit of going against the grain of your thinking can bring you back from despair and install confidence. Be kind to yourself. Dedicate some time each day to think positively. You can focus on recalling good memories or visualizing your goals.

Martin Seligman who is a leader in positive psychology is famous for saying "One of the most significant findings in psychology in the last twenty years is that individuals can choose the way they think." Additional studies from The University of Michigan concluded that organizations which have high performance rates are more likely to have leaders who make more positive statements. Those positive statements help to build stronger relationships. It's not about sucking up to someone. On the contrary you can be constructive in feedback and focus on building up someone's confidence. There are effective ways to implement positive statements. First of all, make sure they are sincere and authentic. Remain objective in your evaluations both of yourself and of others.

Curate your own positive influences

The reality is that there is so much negativity in the world these days. Just turn on the news and you will be drip fed it all day long. The media and news know that this gets attention and so they push that narrative. Bad news gets views because it plays on our emotions of fear and anger. Those are very powerful emotions and when they are triggered, they can grow like a snowball rolling down a mountain. Eventually this negativity spills over into our lives. But we have to be the gatekeepers of our minds and control what we allow into it. Otherwise, it can slowly corrupt our minds. Resist this negative information. Curate your own positive influences. You don't need to know about murders and shocking crimes on the other side of the world.

Fill your mind with positive influences. It's up to you to make an effort to increase the positivity in your life whilst reducing the negativity. Take a look at how you're spending your time. What kinds of movies or TV do you watch? What kind of music do you listen to? Are those positive influences? Sure, those sad songs can bring back memories of a lost love, but isn't it time to move on? Try something more uplifting. It won't resonate with you at first but give it a shot and stick with it.

Pay attention to what you are consuming. All of these

influences might seem small but it all matters and it will all contribute to a more positive life. In addition to the media, pay attention to the mental images consuming your mind. The way you imagine yourself and your surroundings has an important influence on your thinking. Instead of dwelling on dark and negative thoughts, make an effort to focus on more colorful, light and uplifting thoughts. With enough persistence your mind will start to reject those unnecessary negative thoughts and welcome the positive ones. Remember that you become what you think about most of the time. Start thinking about great things and become someone amazing.

Keep a record of your thoughts and emotions. At the end of the day journal about them. What kinds of emotions and thoughts did you experience that day? Were they mostly positive? Or were they mostly negative? What caused those emotions? What can you do to make them more positive tomorrow? Remember positive thinking will improve your life and health! Therefore, the more you can fill your day with positive emotions the better your days will be.

Imagine your child once again

As I mentioned earlier it is possible to change your outlook on life from a negative to a positive. But it won't happen overnight. That's not real lasting change. No, I'm talking about achieving deep rooted, life lasting change. With daily practice and awareness this is possible. The journey goes on. Imagine your child once again. As children our thoughts are mostly positive. We loved to play and were free from doubts, fears or criticism of ourselves. Imagine how much you are limiting yourself now. Realize that you'll never live your dreams if you have those barriers made by yourself.

Break the barriers. Go after that job or relationship. Don't listen to those doubts that tell you you're not good enough. After all, you're a human on this earth and you deserve a shot as much as everyone else. Pump yourself up and take action. Doing that is not as hard as you think. You just have to do it. Replace those negative thoughts with positive ones. Be in the moment and take action. Action cures everything. You are more than enough. Better than you imagine!

Focus on the positive of every situation and don't take anything personally. Just because someone didn't smile at you. It means nothing. Maybe they are shy. Maybe they are having a bad day. Your inner dialogue is much different from theirs. Be curious, say hi. Take action and explore. Maybe it goes nowhere but you should be proud of yourself for making a move. The more you take action when your mind over thinks the more empowered, confident and positive you will become.

Gratitude

Become more grateful for the life you have. So much has been written about the positive effects of gratitude. Pay attention and make use of it. I like to wake up each morning and write out three things that I am grateful for. Following on I write out why I am grateful and how it makes me feel. Starting your days like this will develop your mind to be more grateful and set your day off on a positive note. Furthermore, you can also do it at the end of the day. Write what you're grateful for that day.

Count your blessings. Instead of being frustrated with yourself try being grateful for recognizing your overthinking. It takes courage to do that. "I am grateful for feeling like this because it allows me to make a change".

When you become more grateful for life and yourself then your thoughts will become more positive. Your mind will be in a much more productive and happy state. Take a deep breath, relax and tune into gratitude.

Self-Esteem

Healthy and happy mental wellness results from a high level of self-esteem and in turn a greater quality of life. Self-esteem is a term used in psychology to describe the overall subjective sense of personal worth or value that a person has of themselves. In simpler terms it can be defined as how much a person likes themselves. This further defines a number of important factors including, confidence, identity, feeling of security, competencies and a sense of belonging. It plays a key role in overthinking. Low self-esteem is perhaps one of the most common reasons for overthinking.

Self-esteem fluctuates throughout our lives. In children it tends to be lowest and increases into adulthood before reaching a relatively stable level. Levels depend on the personality and lifestyle of a particular individual. For example, influences that impact on it include, age, genetics, illness, physical ability, socioeconomic status, thinking and much more. Often our life experiences influence our overall levels of self-esteem. For example, if we are surrounded by negative friends and family then we are likely to have low self-esteem.

When you begin to understand your own self-esteem, it can

help you to strike a well-balanced life. Your relationships, emotional health and decisions are all influenced by self-esteem. That is why it is so important to create a positive view of yourself so that you are inspired by life and always rise to the challenge. Those with healthy levels of self-esteem are great at establishing and maintaining healthy relationships with others. This is because they already have a healthy relationship with themselves. In addition, they are realists who understand themselves and can fully express how they feel.

On the other hand, people who have low self-esteem tend to be much less confident in their abilities and often doubt themselves. As such they constantly struggle with motivation or trying new things because they lack enough belief in themselves. As a result, their relationships suffer and they feel unloved or unworthy.

It's important to note that people can also have too much self-esteem. In that case they end up feeling entitled to certain success or achievements. Yet they don't have the abilities to back it up. Just imagine the trash talking boxer who gets knocked out. Yes, too much self-esteem will cloud your judgement and people will find it difficult to connect with you.

Causes of low self-esteem

As mentioned earlier self-esteem tends to be stable throughout a person's life. But it can change dramatically during your life. Difficult life experiences, stresses and challenges can cause such changes. Those might include.

- Someone abusing you or bullying you

- Prejudice or discrimination against you

- Losing your job or being unable to do your job

- Problems with work or study

- Overall life stress

- Health problems - mental or physical

- Problems with relationships

- Body image concerns

- Financial problems

There are various other reasons or experiences that might not be listed here. Just be aware of the negative vibes and bad influences in your own life. Whatever affects your self-esteem you should remember that it's right for you to still focus on feeling good about yourself. Change can be difficult but with small steps you make improvements.

How to have healthy self-esteem

When you have a healthier level of self-esteem, you're going to be more motivated to go for what you want in life. You will also have the benefit of healthier relationships. Not just with others but also with yourself. Clearly having a higher self-esteem is a way to not only feel better about ourselves but also to become more resilient to overthinking.

Following on are some really simple ways to improve your self-esteem.

Feel confident or fake it till you make it

True you might not feel like a particularly happy person right now. Overthinking has its hold on you and life just isn't going your way. When it rains ask, "is the best you have got to throw at me? Because I'm stronger!" Look on the positive side of things. Believe in yourself, no one is better or worse than you. We all have our own setbacks and version of life. Realize that you don't know what someone had to go through to get there and they don't know the same of you. So, stop comparing. Believe it. If that seems so hard then just act confident and fake, it until you feel it. Stick your head up and push your shoulders back. Stand up straight. Do things in a confident and calm manner. Take your time and don't rush things. Savor each moment and live it to the max. Change your behavior and your thinking will change also.

Say no if you don't want to

Healthy self-esteem comes from strong values and boundaries. If you don't want to do something, then say no. Problem is many of us take on too many responsibilities. We find it difficult to say no. Sometimes we just need to practice being able to say no or to delegate those tasks. Practice this skill. There are going to be times when you're asked to do something you prefer not to. Have the courage to say no. Trust me, you will get stronger with practice.

Stop dwelling on any past regrets or negative experiences

Be aware of your negative thoughts, identify them, challenge them and then change them. All of us have made mistakes in the past. The things we regret. The stupid things we said. The stupid things we did. But the past is in the past my friend and you cannot change it. Only can you change your perception of it. Instead of dwelling on the negatives of the past try to look at what you can learn. Switch from a victim to a victor.

Positive affirmations

Practice positive self-talk. Try reciting affirmations to yourself. Affirmations have become very popular in recent times. But most are not really effective because they have a critical problem. That is, they make people feel low self-worth. This is due to the fact that the affirmations they use are too far from their existing beliefs. For example, if your flat broke and you affirm that you're a millionaire then you're going to on some level realize it is just not true. Start where you're at and aim a bit higher. Be practical and make them believable. For example, instead of saying "I'm a millionaire" you could say "I am on the path to riches". Or I am making "ten grand a month". Simply make them more believable.

Have a bunch of empowering affirmations that you can recite when you wake up and say before bed. In fact, say them whenever you feel like a nice boost. Keep at it and you will witness the results. Then you can keep on upgrading your affirmations as you fuel and grow your level of self-esteem.

Grow your strengths and work on your weaknesses

Self-esteem is grown by demonstrating your abilities and achievements. If you're good at something the more your belief in it grows. Figure out what your strengths are and do more of it. If you're a great cook, then cook more. If you love lifting weights, then do that more and so on. The confidence in your beliefs will spill over into your levels of self-esteem. All in all, it's a positive building cycle. Do what you love and watch your self-esteem grow.

At the same time find what your weak areas are. Work on improving them. You can start small just like the first time you rode a bicycle. Then when you become more comfortable again your self-esteem grows. Be gentle and take it slow.

Forgive yourself when you make a mistake. When it feels like you're not going anywhere, don't give up. Draw strength from your victories and keep growing.

Be your own best friend

When feeling bad about yourself it can be hard to accept a compliment. It feels like the person is joking with you. The next time someone compliments you, take it as a truth and be thankful for it. Prepare yourself in advance to thank them with words and a smile. Feel the emotions of praise. Stop judging yourself and being critical. If you were your own best friend, you wouldn't behave in such a way. Start being your own best friend.

Improving your self-esteem will require some work. But in doing so you're building more healthy emotions and habits. The return on your investment will be worth it.

The Hierarchy of Needs

Abraham Maslow was famous for writing about the hierarchy of needs. Self-esteem plays an important role in the hierarchy of needs. It is one of the most basic of human motivations and is found at level four of the hierarchy of needs. We need appreciation from others and self-respect in order to experience healthy self-esteem. In turn both needs must be satisfied in order for us to reach the highest level of self-actualization.

The hierarchy of needs explains that human motivation is based on pursuing different levels of needs. Those needs are set in a hierarchical order which humans are intrinsically motivated by. The order begins with covering the most basic of needs before moving on to more advanced needs.

Level1: Physiological Needs
Physiological needs are at the bottom level of the hierarchy of

needs. These concern the essentials of human survival. Those are things such as the need for water, food, shelter, rest health and so on. A person is motivated by this level in order to survive.

Level 2: Safety Needs

Safety needs are at the second level of the hierarchy of needs. A person needs to feel safe and secure within their environment. The motivation for law and order comes from unpredictable and dangerous conditions. People need protection from the elements, violence, sickness and so on. They also need job security, savings and income.

Level 3: Love and Belonging Needs

Love and Belonging needs are at the second level of the hierarchy of needs. Humans are social beings that feed off of interaction with others. We all need friendships, family and love. Our desire is to feel wanted and to give love. Without it we might experience depression or loneliness.

Level 4: Self-Esteem Needs

Self-Esteem needs are at the second level of the hierarchy of needs. Those are related to the human need to gain status, respect and recognition. With love and belonging needs fulfilled we seek to fulfill our self-esteem needs. This can be broken into two categories. The need for others' respect and the need for self-respect. The respect from others concerns concepts such as recognition, fame, prestige, and so on. Whilst self-respect needs concerns to confidence, dignity, competence, freedom and so on.

Level 5: Self-Actualization Needs

The final level of the hierarchy of needs is self-actualization needs. This is when an individual reaches their full potential. At this level they become the best version of themselves. This can manifest in ways such as education, skills development, fulfilling life dreams, pursuing happiness, love and so on. It could even mean becoming the best parent or a best friend. In general, it is the pursuit of excellence.

Now we have explored the perils of negativity and washed ourselves with positivity. Arriving at this point we have a fairly clean slate or new foundation to build up our minds. Let's now look at some powerful tools and mindsets in the next chapters.

MEDITATION & MINDFULNESS

Meditation

Meditation as it is most commonly known is the practice of training attention. Most people assume that meditation is something practiced in a temple with a monk sat cross legged on a cushion. But it doesn't have to be that way. It can be as simple as a state of mind. For example, when we are doing something, we give it our full attention in the moment. Washing the dishes can be a mediation. Walking can be a meditation. Mainstream practices involve taking the time out to sit down, close your eyes and focus on your breathing as it goes in and out. Inevitably thoughts will arise, but as you notice yourself getting distracted by them you gently bring your attention back to your breathing.

Mediation has been proven again and again by countless studies that conclude it improves focus and brain function. All you need is ten minutes a day and you can begin to reap the rewards almost immediately. The amazing thing about mediation is that it spills over into your daily living. After some weeks of daily meditation, you will start to notice that food tastes better, you see more clearly and life is less stressful. This is because meditation is calming down your internal dialogue and allowing you to be in the moment experiencing life at its fullest.

Mediation has grown in popularity over the last few decades. What was once just something practiced by monks has now become a commercial success. Meditation groups have surged in popularity and even the business world has picked up on it. Of course, meditation isn't some magic pill that cures everything in your life. But it will provide some much-needed space. Here are some excellent reasons to meditate.

- Self-awareness

- Stress relief

- Connect with life

- Better focus

- Less brain chatters

Meditation and overthinking

Overthinking takes over your mind and can lead to doubt, suspicion, and overall bad mind states. Overthinking is a big issue for many of us. We admire thinkers such as Shakespeare, Darwin and Einstein who have changed the world with their thinking. That type of thinking is a positive trait, but overthinking is not. Essentially overthinking is a tidal wave of random unhelpful thoughts. Now that won't help you or bring you peace. However, meditation is something that can help to resolve overthinking and bring peace to your life.

Meditation can help you to gain perspective and see the larger picture of life. In turn that leads to a more peaceful and happy life. Seeking out a higher state of consciousness will help you to overcome your negative thoughts and declutter your mind. Dealing with life in a more organized and calm way without getting distracted from your purpose and happiness. Plus, you will be free from attachment. So many benefits.

Meditation and the brain

In 2005 Sara Lazar, a Harvard neuroscientist published some astonishing research about mediation. She found that meditation can literally change the brain structure by thickening parts of the cortex that are responsible for controlling attention and emotion. In a little as eight weeks of practicing, daily half hour meditation this brain change is possible.

Further studies in 2014 found that the brains of meditators had enlarged regions. Those included the insula which is responsible for emotional self-awareness and also parts of the cingulate cortex, orbitofrontal cortex and prefrontal cortex. These are responsible for self-regulation and attention. It is no wonder that experienced meditators are better at focusing and struggle less with stress, worry, anxiety or overthinking. Various other studies have proven that meditation can change our neural circuitry which makes us more compassionate and more likely to experience positive feelings.

Not only does meditation change internal emotional states as a result it also changes our behavior. One study in particular concluded that people after being trained in mediation for just two weeks were more likely to make charitable donations. Whilst another study discovered that people who meditated are more likely to offer a chair to someone who needs it.

There are five regions of the brain associated with healthy function which are substantially affected by meditation.

The Left Hippocampus

This area of the brain is responsible for helping us to learn. Cognitive ability and memory are found here in addition to emotional regulators that are responsible for empathy and self-awareness. Various research has concluded that the cortical thickness of this area grows when a person mediates daily. As the density increases those important functions are improved.

The Posterior Cingulate

This area of the brain is associated with self-relevance and wandering thoughts. It considers how one subjectively refers to oneself as they process information. The stronger and larger this is the less the mind will tend to wonder. In turn the more realistic a sense of self will be. Since meditation trains the mind to remain in the present moment it directly benefits the posterior cingulate which increases its density.

The Pons

This area of the brain is a very busy and important part that hosts many neurotransmitters which regulate brain activity. It can be found in the middle of the brain stem and that's where the name pons comes from which is the Latin word for "bridge." A number of essential brain functions are attributed to the pons. Those include facial expressions, sleep, physical function, sensory input and more. Meditation has been found to strengthen the pons.

The Temporo Parietal Junction (TPJ)

The TPJ is associated with compassion, empathy and our sense of perspective. Whilst the posterior cingulate focuses on "me", the TPJ focuses on everything else. When we consider things from another perspective The TPJ becomes more active. The benefits of meditation such as lowering stress, anxiety and putting us more in the present moment combine to create a stronger TPJ. This can help us to become better people since we have improved empathy and compassion.

The Amygdala

This area of the brain is responsible for producing anxiety, fear and stress. This is the threat detection area of the brain. When it perceives a potential threat, it will trigger or fight or flight response. This then releases the stress hormones which include cortisol and adrenaline. This causes us to get fixated on the threat and make it hard for us to break free and focus on anything else. In the brains of meditators, it is physically smaller. Reducing this size is great because as a result we are going to be less sensitive to negative emotions. It's no wonder we feel better with a daily dose of meditation.

In a 2012 study people who had never mediated before were trained for eight weeks of mediation. Before they started the training they had MRIs, scans to discover where their brain activity was occurring. Whilst they were being scanned, they were shown upsetting images. After the eight weeks of meditation training, they were shown those images again whilst under the MRI scanner. This time their brain activity showed a reduction in the amygdala. One of the most amazing things about the 2012 study was that the reduction of amygdala activity continued even when the participants went back to their baseline state. This further proves that meditation can result in lasting mental changes.

How to Meditate

Now with all that being said one more thing needs to be explained. You won't change your brain unless you sit down and do your daily meditation! Sure, some days you won't want to. Everything else is way more important. Push on and stick with it, even on the bad days. The practice is very straightforward and easy to do.

To begin with, find a comfortable place to sit and relax. It should be free from distraction and comfortable. You can choose to lie down or sit as you please. The best results tend to be seated cross legged. Strike a balance between alert and comfortable. Choose a time that works for you. At the start of the day or in the evening are the best times. Set a timer for ten minutes at first. As you become more comfortable with the mediation you can build up to longer sessions

Setting aside a time each day is an effective way to establish a consistent meditation routine. With daily practice you will become more accustomed and comfortable with that practice. All it requires is just a few minutes a day. That can make a huge difference in your day-to-day life. I know we all have busy lives, and it does require taking time out of your day. But the busier you are the more important it is. With mediation you will become a more effective person because it will stimulate long lasting benefits into our lives. From reduced stress levels, awareness with ourselves and greater connection with life.

So how do you actually mediate? There are many ways to meditate. Most of those are beyond the scope of this book. But here I will outline a simple mindfulness meditation. Primarily this is about learning to focus on your breathing. As each breath goes in and out, notice how your mind tends to wander from the task. The muscles of mindfulness and attention are built by practicing returning your focus to your breathing. When you learn to pay attention to your breathing it anchors you into the present moment. Here and now without judgement.

It sounds simple and easy to do but it requires patience and discipline. Our minds have been burned out by all the distractions and information nowadays that something so simple has become so challenging.

Follow this step-by-step process to meditate
Step one

Find a comfortable place to sit. You should strike a balance between comfort and alertness. Laying down would be too much comfort. You might fall asleep. Whilst standing would be too alert and not enough comfort. Sitting on a seat or cross legged on a cushion is good. You can do this with eyes closed or open. Go with what gives you the most present feeling.

Step two

Set a time. In the beginning you can set an alarm to go off after five to ten minutes. As you get more comfortable and experienced, try longer times. Twenty minutes is optimal. Oh, and remember to turn your phone off and make sure you have no other distractions. Start the timer.

Step three

Notice your body. Scan your attention across your body and pay attention to each area. Move around if you need to at first to make sure you're comfortable. Then stay in that position.

Step four

Focus on your breathing. Begin by counting to ten and focusing on your breathing. Follow the sensations of your breathing as each breath goes in and out. Notice all of the smallest details from the air filling your lungs to passing your lips. You will notice moments of pure presence. That is pure consciousness. You will know when it happens. No thinking just in the moment.

Let go and just be with your breathing. Thoughts will run through your mind but when you catch yourself caught up in them forgive yourself and return to focusing on your breathing. Allow your mind to relax into the moment and experience consciousness.

Step five

Notice anytime your mind wanders from focusing on your breathing. This is natural and will inevitably happen. When you notice, this has happened forgive yourself and thank yourself that you are coming back to the present moment. Return your attention to your breathing. Don't be hard on yourself for it. Simply return back to your breathing.

Step six

When the timer goes off gently open your eyes if they are closed. Stretch your body and take a moment to notice your environment, thoughts and emotions. Give thanks for the moment.

As you can see meditation is pretty simple to do. The best results come from committing to doing it every day. No days off. Even when you do not feel like doing it, stick with it. It's a beautiful thing and the more you practice the more you will fall in love with it.

Walking meditation

Walking meditation is another great meditation practice. Find a place that has plenty of space. It's great if the floor has lots of texture to it. Remove your shoes so that you can feel the details of the floor in your feet. Begin to walk slowly. With each step focus on the experience of walking and the sensations it brings. When you reach the end of your path, start again until you have completed the time you want to meditate.

*Important: Remind yourself to meditate

Make meditation a part of your morning or evening routine. I personally practice after reading in the morning. This works because I stack my habits. Doing one habit triggers a cue to do the next and so on. In the evenings I also meditate. My cue is arriving home or taking an evening shower. Then I meditate and journal after. Use physical reminders such as a yoga mat or a cushion in your room. Put reminders on your phone or even stick-up post notes in your home. Every time you see any of those it will remind you to meditate. Stick with it.

Mindfulness

Scientists estimate that up to ninety five percent of human behavior is on autopilot. Functioning in such a hectic world relies on habitual behaviors. Shortcuts established in the neural networks of our brains help us complete various activities on autopilot. Problem is our brain might sometimes think it knows what is best for us which can cause us to relapse into bad behaviors. But as discussed earlier in this book much of that is coming from our primitive brain. We need to get back in the driver seat. Our intention must be stronger, and we need control to achieve that.

Mindfulness is a powerful method of counteracting this primitive type of thinking. It is the opposite of autopilot behavior. Instead, it is direct control of your actions and decisions. But it's not something that comes easily. The process will require you to rewire your brain from mental clutter of the past or future and to instead focus on the present moment. This is a mode of behavior that requires practice to activate our brains and make them stronger. With practice we stimulate our brains neuroplasticity and activate grey matter. In turn new neurons are formed and stronger pathways are built.

Truly it is a simple but incredibly powerful concept that can be utilized at any time. From during the most mundane of activities to during the most thrilling. In a mindful state you will no longer be attached to or be a victim of your thoughts. The result is simply being present in whatever you're doing at that time and experiencing it fully. Building the habit is what is challenging. However, if you're willing to make a change and start practicing mindfulness then it will become easier to adopt this new concept. There are also some key habits you can utilize to welcome a more mindful state.

First you need to be prepared to have an open mind to new suggestions. Such new ideas will require change to defeat those bad habits which are creating chaos and confusion in your mind. Make an effort to regularly spend time cleaning your mind of overwhelming or obsessive thoughts. Otherwise, those thoughts can linger around in your mind and negatively affect your emotions. Are you ready to clear away brain fog and reduce the noise of mental chatter?

How to practice mindfulness
Practicing mindfulness is all about directing your attention to the details of daily life. It won't require you to take a class or

sit in uncomfortable positions for hours. Everything you have is already within you right now. Instead of being stressed out or anxious we take time to enjoy each moment and sensation of the moment. Turn the volume of your mind down and bring your awareness back to your body.

"Mindfulness is awareness that arises through paying attention, on purpose, in the present moment, non-judgmentally," Jon Kabat-Zinn, creator of the program Mindfulness-Based Stress Reduction (MBSR)

Just like a seed grows when watered, mindfulness also grows through the water of consistent practice. Regular practice will help you to overcome overthinking and break free from negative emotions. Set aside time each day to be mindful. Every moment you have it is available to you. It can be as simple as scanning your body or breathwork.

Body scan

A body scan involves you paying attention to each part of your body from your head to toes. Take a moment. You could be sitting in traffic. Focus. Begin at the point of your toes. Bring your awareness to them. Shift to your heels, then to your ankles, lower legs and up to the top of your head. Notice and pay awareness to each part.

It can help to lay down on your back. Have your legs laid out in front of you and arms at the sides with the palms faced upwards. Start to focus your attention onto the individual parts of your body. Go slowly and deliberately. Become aware of the sensations, thoughts and emotions associated with each body part.

Meditation

Mediation is the ultimate practice of mindfulness. Setting aside time to practice consistently each day will naturally make you more mindful. It's like a byproduct of the mediation. You become more mindful during each day. Try out seated or walking meditation. For more information on practicing meditation see the earlier part of this chapter.

Breathwork

Breathing triggers, the parasympathetic nervous system which results in more calmness. Similar to meditation, breathwork or conscious breathing is another tool we can use to ground ourselves. Take deep measured breaths into your diaphragm. Count them as they go in and out. This lowers your stress and anxiety. Next time you feel stressed out, start doing some deep breathing. Focus completely on the details of your breathing. As it enters your body and exhales. Count all the way. Allow your breathing to bring peace back to you.

Remember that mindfulness isn't about silencing your mind. The goal is to become aware of the present moment without judgement. It's natural to make judgements as situations and events arise. When you become aware just make a mental note and let them pass you by like leaves in the wind. Stay in the present moment and just observe. Your mind will try to carry you away in the wind, but you stay grounded in the present. Whenever your mind begins to wander, practice recognizing when it happens. Forgive yourself if you get distracted. It's normal, just gently come back to the present moment.

Take the time to enjoy the experience of life. Immerse yourself in the moment. When you touch, see, smell and taste. Take the time to enjoy it all and live fully in the moment. You'll find there is so much joy to be found even in the simplest of pleasures. The more you practice mindfulness the stronger it gets. Think of it as connecting with and taking care of yourself.

Now let's explore some more techniques, tactics and mind states to deal with overthinking.

MORE TECHNIQUES, TACTICS & MINDSETS

Finally, you have some time out to yourself. Only then your mind starts overthinking! What about that email I was supposed to send? Why did I say that to her? What should I wear tomorrow? Does any of this sound familiar? Forgive yourself because it's all part of the experience of being a human.

Train your brain. Retrain it to think differently with the correct practices. When you pay attention to your thinking it will help you to become aware of any bad mental habits. Through building healthier habits, you will build stronger mental muscles to become a better person and one who is freer from overthinking. In this chapter I will give you some more techniques, tactics and mindsets that can help to deal with your overthinking.

Self-awareness

Realize when you're overthinking. For some of us this might prove to be difficult because it has become so normal. Self-awareness is one of the most important ways to change your mindset. The next time you find yourself overthinking take a step back and become aware of it.

"We suffer more in imagination than in reality", Lucius Annaeus Seneca

Close your eyes and take a deep breath. Become aware of your feelings, thoughts and emotions. This is the first step you need to take. Now that you're self-aware you can focus on cooling down. Find a comfortable place. Turn off any distracting or stimulating things. If there is music on, switch it off or put on something more chilled out. Turn your phone data off. In fact, get away from any screens. Going outside into some nature would be ideal. Maybe sit down in the park or go for a walk outside. Pay attention to your body. Relax your posture. Breathe deeply in and slowly out. Stay here in the present moment. Again meditation, prayer and mindfulness can help you stimulate this.

Stop trying to fight your thoughts. This may sound counterintuitive but the effective way to really stop persistent unwanted thoughts is to first observe them in a curious and non-judgmental way. This alone may help to decrease their intensity. For example, if I told you not to think of a pink elephant, you're probably going to think of one. The same is true with those persistent thoughts. When you try to stop them, it usually makes it worse. Just allow them, and they will dissipate eventually.

Be kind

Be a kind person. Empathy and thinking from another perspective will help you greatly here. If your overthinking stems from interactions or thoughts of other people, then it can be a great idea to first of all thinks about things from the other person's perspective. How we see the world is shaped by our own values, assumptions and life experiences. When you imagine that viewpoint from someone else it can help you to break through mental noise.

The world is a huge place, and most people are focused on their own journey. The truth is they probably are not really thinking that much about you. But we have become so reliant on the opinions of others. We are willing to spend so much time thinking about how much they value our self-worth or if they approve of us. It's almost as if our identity has become no longer a reflection of ourselves but rather a conformity to others. Our fears trick us into thinking things and opinions don't exist.

Do nice things for other people. When you see the opportunity to help others, do it. It doesn't have to be any grand gestures. Every little help. Send those ripples of kindness out into the world. Maybe your neighbor needs a lift. Give that stranger a smile. Tip the waiter. Pick up some trash. Be sincere in your efforts.

Remember to also be kind to yourself as well. Dwelling on past mistakes won't help. Stop beating yourself up, learn and let go. If you need a friend to talk to then reach out to your social circle, family or even a qualified therapist.

Questions

Let your thoughts have their voice. Listen to them. Once you have heard them, begin to question them. Ask yourself;

- Is this helping me?

- What would be a better way to think?

- What are the consequences?

- Is there a better solution?

- If this were my last day on earth, would I think like this?

Have these questions written out. There was a time in my life when I was plagued by overthinking. To retrain my brain, I had lists of questions written out on my phone. Whenever I was faced with a long period of time to myself, I would read them over one by one and answer each. Usually, I would do this aloud. It truly reframed my thinking to become more constructive.

These questions were gathered over time, and it took me about thirty to sixty minutes to go over all of them. I used to work a night shift and during the last hour I had almost nothing to do. Typically, my mind would start going into depressed negative thinking as a default. Because life is like a slippery slope and the devil is always grabbing at your ankles. You have to keep pushing up or it will drag you down. So, at that time I decided to take hold of the reins of my destiny. The questions I had were all conducive to state changing. They had to have that effect. I would Google for questions to ask yourself or state changing questions. Things like that. You will find tons of those "fifty questions to ask yourself" and so on. I saved any that resonated with me. They had to inspire me. They would also have a follow up question. For each area of my life I had questions. For example,

- What am I proud of? What about that makes me proud?

- How is this situation making me stronger? How is that going to make me feel?

- Who do I love? Who loves me?

- How do I want to wake up feeling? Why?

- What's the best way to spend my time? How could I make it better?

Focus on solutions. Questions will give you the solutions. Dwelling on your problems will not help you. It can be easy to get carried away with negative thoughts. Take responsibility.

Think Big

The Magic Art of Thinking Big is a world-famous classic book. One of the most useful messages in that book is to take time out each day to Think Big. Some of the most powerful and influential people in the world are known for practicing this. From presidents to billionaires to athletes. Time for reflection is essential to their development and success.

Instead of stewing on your problems, take time to focus on thinking of solutions. Use your questions to get your thinking going in the right direction. Block off at least thirty minutes a day to just sit down and think big. There should be no diastricons present. No phone or technology. You could go for a walk and do this. Sometimes your mind just needs to unwind and rewire itself a little. Kind of like formatting a hard drive. Sometimes you might want to think of a particular goal or challenge you are facing. Think about it from different angles. Or sometimes you can think big about your future and how you plan to succeed.

Think of the big picture. For the most part overthinking is a great big mess of small and meaningless thoughts. When you catch yourself overthinking, consider the bigger picture. How will these thoughts and issues affect you in the next five to ten years? Will they really matter? I doubt it. So therefore, don't waste too much mental energy on them.

Think big and prime your brain to become more powerful. The human brain is incredibly adaptive. It can learn to adapt to new challenges and ways of thinking. This can happen incredibly fast. The act of taking time to think constructively will prime your brain to become more powerful. Use it to your advantage and unlock your full potential.

Distraction

The lure of overthinking can be so strong. Research has shown that distraction can help us to break free from overthinking. Choose activities that are highly engaging and positive; it can be a strong remedy. Good examples include puzzles, vigorous exercise, dancing or playing a strategic game. Those will be effective at shifting your attention from overthinking.

Most people associate distraction with being something

negative, but it can be a healthy distraction such as going to play sports, gardening or going for a walk and so on. Replace overthinking with an activity that you enjoy. Be in the moment with the activity. That could be anything from cooking to exercise to making love. Or it could be getting up and going for a walk. It could even be something within your mind such as replaying a great memory. The key is to find distractions that are positive and put you in the present moment.

Philosophical razors

In philosophy there are principles known as razors which can help you to shave off any bad thinking. Two major philosophical razors provide wisdom to avoid overthinking.

Occam's razor

The principle of Occam's razor states that when there are two explanations for an event the simple one is the most likely cause. For example, when you have to make more assumptions the more unlikely a reason becomes. This can help you to overcome overthinking that comes from past fears.

Hanlon's razor

The principle of Hanlon's razor steam from Occam's razor.

This suggests that avoiding any assumption of wrong intentions, stupidity, incompetence, or error could explain the cause. Therefore, any chances of an event happening because of bad intentions are far less likely. Understanding this will help you to stop get caught up in overthinking caused by the assumption of bad intentions.

Change your stories

Tony Robbins is one of the most famous self-help gurus ever. This particular method was suggested by the man himself. Our mind is full of stories that we choose to tell about ourselves. For example, your date is twenty minutes late and she hasn't replied to your messages. You can tell yourself any of the following examples of stories:

She isn't coming

Or

She probably goes delayed

Or another example. Your boss didn't respond to your email about a potential raise. You can tell yourself any of the following examples of stories:

He isn't going to give me a raise

Or

Maybe he didn't have time to reply

It's up to you to change your stories so that they are more positive and stop you from overthinking. Until you do that, you're more likely to fall into panic attacks, anxiety and overthinking. Instead, why not manage your stories? Think about it. Do your stories empower you or hold you back? Maybe you tell yourself that

"I always worry too much"

Or

"I'm not good enough"

To overcome these stories and beliefs you first of all need to identify them. When these scenarios come up, write down the first thoughts you have. Notice that there will be themes popping up. Start working on replacing them with more positive and empowering stories. When you change your story, your life will change for the better.

Exercise

Exercising is an excellent way of countering stress, anxiety and overthinking before it happens. Healthy body equals a healthy mind and vice versa. I have pushed this many times in this book because of its high importance. Exercise gives us a welcome distraction or break from overthinking. Take the time out each day to practice some physical exercise. It should be challenging enough to keep you engaged but not too challenging to put you off. You should feel like you're making progress whilst gaining a healthier body. There are so many videos on YouTube to learn about exercising. Or you could join a local fitness club or gym.

Go out into nature or for a walk. When your mind won't stop and overthinking is driving you crazy, step outside into nature or go for a walk. It will help you to restore mental clarity and gain a new perspective. If you're out in nature you will be humbled and inspired by the beauty. Your overthinking will subside as you take in your surroundings. Try to go for daily walks and if you can't look at some pictures of nature. Let it inspire you. Stay active and healthy. In addition, eat a healthy, clean and nutritional diet. This will optimize the functions of your body since they are provided with quality fuel.

Journaling

The Harvard Medical School studied the effects of expressive writing (journaling thoughts and emotions) and they found that it can effectively clear your mind. Simply put it is a way of expressing yourself through writing. Think of it like talking to a friend. This is highly effective at making sense of and processing your thoughts. Having them written out relieves your mind. In addition, it will help you to organize your thoughts and understand your emotions. It makes complete sense to add this to your daily routine. All it requires is five minutes. Journal about your day or anything that bothers you. Think of it as a mental brain dump.

If there are thoughts swirling around in your head, write them down. Investigate each one and question how true they are. Journaling is an excellent relaxation exercise that will also give you valuable insights. Identify and record your thoughts in your journal. Actively work on trying to change them for the better. Get to the root of the cause of any bad feelings. Use your notebook to help you search inside. When you dig into the details and evaluate your thinking you can work on making a positive change.

Every day we are inundated with information, and we need to take time out to process it. If something has been stuck in your head, get it out onto the paper. Free your mind. Do this without judging yourself. You're the only one who is going to read it and so it doesn't need to be grammatically correct or flow like Shakespeare. At the end of the week, you can go over your notes, review them and gain strength. I'm sure over time you will notice recurring themes. Take action on those.

In addition to tracking your negative thoughts, be sure to also acknowledge your successes. Praise yourself when you do something well. Write out the things you did well and what you're grateful for. It doesn't have to be something huge. Simple things. Let them add up.

Set goals and stick to them

Life is here for you. Why not live it to the fullest? Dare to dream. What would you like to achieve in this life? Where do you see yourself in five years? How do you want to feel? What kind of relationship would you like to have? How much money do you want to make? What kind of experiences do you want to have? Ask yourself questions to find out what your goals are. Set goals for the near future in say one month, goals for midterm in say six months to one year and long-term goals for five years or more. Stack the importance and make plans to achieve them.

Having clearly defined goals with plans will reduce overthinking. Since you know what your purpose and goals are it will mean you're less likely to get distracted or caught up in overthinking. Have your goals written out and everyday check them. I personally have a spreadsheet of them and in addition every morning I write them out. It takes less than ten minutes, but it puts my mind into the right focus. The reticular activating system (RAS) is a set of nerves within our brain which serves to filter out unnecessary information allowing only the important through. It is the reason why when you learn a new word you begin to hear it everywhere. Or when someone says your name in a crowd your attention immediately snaps to it.

With clearly defined goals we are more likely to stay on track and do the right things. Our RAS ensures that. Have lists of your goals and the actions you need to take each day, week, month, year and so on. Be organized and purposeful. Having this kind of meaning to your life will reduce the amount of overwhelm and overthinking since most of it will not matter. Peace and focus will become your new mind states now that you have purpose.

Mental Toughness

When thinking of mental toughness, you probably imagine a navy seal or commander fearless and stoic. Essentially, mental toughness is a positive set of mental attributes that help a person to deal with challenging situations. In short it is a person's ability to resist, deal with and overcome any worries, overthinking, doubts or concerns that are preventing success. Of course, this is a great remedy for overthinking. Those with mental toughness are much less likely to engage in self-doubt, worry or overthinking.

The concept of mental toughness originated from sports training and psychology to help elite athletes perform better. The studies emerged in the mid-1980s and have continued to this day. Dr. Jim Loehr, a famous performance psychologist, is one of the originators of pioneering mental toughness. Recently the term has acquired a broader use in business, sports and coaches. These days it is used by business professionals, performers and athletes to achieve groundbreaking results. For athletes it has helped them to become better and cope with the challenges of training and competition.

A number of studies have directly linked mental toughness to sporting success and achievements. There are several reasons that contribute to mental toughness influencing success. In the case of sports, athletes need to be able to believe in themselves whilst handling pressure and avoiding negative distractions. Their desire to win must be so strong that it overcomes any other smaller desires. Mental toughness is what will set them apart from the other athletes. The same can be said in business and life. If you have the mental toughness to believe in yourself, avoid distractions and handle pressure then you are likely to achieve great success.

With a natural or trained psychological edge of mental toughness it will enable you to much more effectively deal with the challenges and demands of pursuing your goals. That could be in the office, gym or at home. Under times of pressure, it will help you become more consistent, focused, confident and controlled. The skill of mental toughness is a valuable asset in all areas of life. Those who train it increase their chances of rising to higher levels of success and excelling in life.

Incidentally mental toughness should be learned and developed by anyone who wishes to improve themselves and produce higher level results. Whether that is in work, sports or life. It can all be applied. Business people, sales teams and entrepreneurs will benefit in big ways from it because they are typically working in high pressure environments. Mental toughness would help them to overcome challenges, believe they can do it and stay focused on achieving their goals. In sports of course mental toughness is a key component towards success.

Lastly, it could help in many areas of your personal life. Maybe you're in a difficult relationship and you need to keep believing in it and have the courage to take the first step towards fixing it. Mental toughness again will help you here. For parents it's great too. Children of any age can put a huge level of stress on parents. It will help you to deal with the challenges, pressures and stress of being a parent.

Can mental toughness be learned?

Yes, there are a number of ways to learn mental toughness. To begin, start reading more about it. A great primer would be the books and research by Dr Jim Loehr. "Mentally Tough" and "Toughness Training For Life" are both great primers on the subject.

Just like a muscle, mental toughness needs to be exercised so that it can grow. This needs to be done consistently and you need to push your limits. Showing up at the gym once a week won't get you decent results. Neither will you get results if you stick with the same weights. Pushing yourself through the difficulty is when you grow and gain stronger mental toughness. For example, you set out to do nine reps on the weights bench. Push for that one more rep! Or you're working on a business task. You're getting tired and want to eat a snack. Push for thirty minutes more of work.

Expanding your comfort zone and going beyond what you thought was possible will make you stronger. Working with others who are achieving at a higher level than you are also great for this. Often when we are alone, we let the pressure off and don't really reach our limits. Having a high achiever around you will help you to break some of your own limits. If you can't find that person, then read biographies of people who overcame huge obstacles to achieve amazing things. I recommend the biography of the greatest boxer of all time, Muhammad Ali. He refused to serve in the war against Vietnam because he didn't believe in it. The U.S government stripped him of his titles for four years and banned him from boxing. Against all odds, he came back four years later and won his titles back.

There will be days when you don't feel like doing anything. Motivation comes and goes. But when it's not there is when your mental toughness kicks in. Build consistent empowering habits and the tough times will become easier because it is a pattern of behavior. The easy way is the hard way. Be consistent and develop a positive mindset. This is the first thing you need to do to increase mental toughness. As we now know the mind is filled with thoughts and most of those are repeated or negative. It's like a huge weight on your back, pulling you down. Trying to achieve something with that extra weight on you is only going to make things more difficult. Why not dump that extra weight and save your strength for the most useful challenges?

Let go of any self-limiting beliefs

Those are just holding you back. If we allow these self-limiting beliefs to control our minds that it overwhelms our ability to think positively. Become aware of your self-limiting beliefs. Take note of them. Question if they are helping you. Question if they are true. Reframe them in a positive way. Affirm those new beliefs.

Break free from all or nothing thinking

This is another form of negative thinking that is crowding your mind with useless negativity. Recognize this as when you're thinking in extremes. For example, you are either great or you are a loser. You either did well or you suck. It's very black and white thinking that is not helping you.

In the real world it can play out like this. Say you wanted to earn $5000 in a month, but you earned $4700. In that case then you're not a loser. Because you gained, you did well! Or you wanted to bench press 120kg, but you hit 115kg. Still a great effort. Shoot for the stars and reach the moon. Don't allow this all or nothing thinning to corrupt your mind. Be grateful for the in between. All those other shades of success. Focus on the positive. Be constructive in your self-criticism and make sure it is acknowledging your success and being constructive towards improvement.

Stop dwelling on the negative. When you dwell on negatives it is wasting more mental energy that could be used in a positive direction. If you want to become mentally tougher then you have to ditch the dwelling. Move on from your failures. Learn from them. Think higher about the future. Expect good things. When things don't work out for you or you face a challenge, sure you can allow yourself to feel disappointment or frustration. That is a normal reaction. Just try to reduce the amount of time that you spend dwelling on it. Be constructive. Seek advice from other people to get a new perspective. Set yourself a time limit to think constructively about it. Journal about it and get it out there on paper. Calm yourself down and examine it with a clear mind. The quicker you can get over this and achieve a solution the quicker you can move towards achieving the success you want in your life.

Connect with your life purpose

A critical element of mental toughness is to have a strong and focused mind. When you have a strong reason or rather a strong life purpose then it will keep you from getting distracted, discouraged or sidetracked from your mission. When that setback comes you figure out a way forward. Usually when we get thrown off, we give up. That's not about willpower or discipline. It's just about having strong enough reasons to keep going.

When the going gets tough the tough get going. When things get tough people usually will escape to work on something easier. But for mentally tough people they will dig in and try to keep going. This is life. It will throw challenges at you. Those will require courage, resilience and mental toughness. Most of that comes down to being a consistent person. If you keep showing up it gets easier because you get stronger. Learn to have a hard-working ethic. Put in the effort daily and become consistent with it. You will be able to deal with those challenges easier when they come up. It rains or you feel tired. No worries, you're already up and ready to go because you were made for this. It's a habit.

"It's not about how hard you hit. It's about how hard you can get hit and keep moving forward. How much you can take and keep moving forward." — Rocky balboa / Sylvester Stallone

No matter who you are, achieving success can be difficult. It will require your physical, mental and emotional energy. You will be faced with ups and downs, failures, burnouts, limiting beliefs, discouragement and much more. With so much stacked against you it can be easy to just quit. Mental toughness is the key to succeeding. It isn't about talent or having passion. It's your ability to stick with something when things become tough. Those who can push beyond obstacles will achieve their dreams. No matter who you are, you can become more mentally tough. No matter who you are, you can push through and achieve your dreams.

"It never gets easier you just get better.", Jordan Hoechlin

CONCLUSION

Here we are at the conclusion of this book about overthinking. I hope that you've discovered some new insights and solutions to dealing with your overthinking. Now that we are here, let's take a moment to summarize the main points and promises.

To begin with we discovered that the human brain has limitless potential and can be much more powerful than even the latest supercomputers. However, we also discovered that we are still falling victim to our primal instincts which haven't evolved since we were being hunted by predators. Clearly those are outdated. The world we now live in is a much safer place. Yet it is such an energetic and abundant place that can be overwhelming. Which causes us to overthink.

With our understanding of our biology and the world around us, my promise then was to explore the root causes of overthinking. Exploring the causes of overthinking was our first step to take towards freedom. Identifying the source is an effective way to get to the root of the problem and to then seek solutions. Beginning with the first cause, stress. For many of us stress is a distinct part of everyday life. Many common causes of stress are affecting us. From stress at work to finances to family to health and to life in general. Stress can affect our behavior, mood, mental and even physical symptoms. With a better understanding of stress, we then explored how to deal with stress.

In brief you should review your lifestyle and build healthy habits. Some of those might include exercise, going to bed at a good time and cutting out any vices or bad influences. If stress from your lifestyle or work is causing your overthinking, then be honest with yourself about the source of it. Reach out for help from friends and colleagues if necessary. They could help you to identify new solutions and perspectives which will help you to take clear steps forward.

The next cause we explored was anxiety. We discovered that anxiety is a normal emotion, and many people feel it on a mild level but it becomes an issue when we're faced with stronger anxiety disorders. Managing anxiety is about getting to the root of the problem and exploring what causes it. Once we've dealt with what the causes are, we can focus on solutions. Those include maintaining good health, focusing on the right things and having an effective system of relaxation.

Following on we explored depression and rumination which affects nearly ten percent of the adult US population. In fact, many people from all over the world suffer from the effects of it. Overthinkers are often left feeling depressed which further submerges into a negative cycle of lowering thoughts. Sleep, eating, concentration and much more are affected by this. Unfortunately, we discovered that there isn't a magic pill or quick fix solution to depression. However, we can learn to effectively deal with it by pushing back on it, challenging our thoughts and having more positive influences in our life. Take action, make plans of things to do with your time and stay connected with your friends and family.

Exploring one more cause of overthinking we explored information overload in our world. In this current age, information is coming at us at hyper speed. Trying to focus or make decisions in such a hectic world has become challenging. Basically, it causes us to overthink. Dealing with such a huge challenge begins with eliminating the non-essential and doing more of what you love. Take accountability for how you spend your time and make sure that you're doing the things that you want to do with the people who you want to be with. In addition, become a more organized person. To be effective you need to remove distractions. Minimalism is a great concept for being more effective and organized. In that chapter we discovered how having less will reduce your mental storage. Then you can focus on what matters. Which in turn leads us to making better decisions. In addition, we identified some other ways to make better decisions. In brief those included setting time limits, using decision models and taking the time out to think.

Next, we looked at managing insomnia naturally without sleeping pills. A common issue for overthinkers is sleep. Not enough, too much or inconsistency. Let it be more natural. Have a consistent sleep schedule. Take enough time to relax before sleep. Finally, we explored medical conditions briefly. Again, let me state that if you suffer from any medical issues then you should seek medical professional advice.

In the next chapter we explored negative thoughts and negativity bias. Evidently some people suffer more than others with negativity. In fact, most people have a leaning towards being more negative. This is known as the negativity bias. In summary humans are prone to leaning towards negative thoughts as an automatic reaction. In this chapter we explored the causes of those negative thoughts. Indeed, negative thoughts can feel incredibly real. We can get lost in them and they can take over our minds. As I mentioned, first of all you need to become aware of your obsessive thoughts. Notice the ones that are not productive and challenge them. It is then that you can work on replacing them with more rational thoughts. With work it will soon become a habit and an evolution of your thinking as it becomes much healthier. Instead of obsessing over negative thoughts the aim will be to develop a new mindset. Instead of being a victim of your thoughts, think what you can do about it.

Take that seriously because that directly affects your health and your immune system. Start to rewire and deal with negative thoughts so that they don't destroy your life.

We explored some simple ways to deal with negative thoughts. Firstly, we looked at acceptance and commitment therapy (ACT). In summary this is a method of reconfiguring your relationship to your thoughts. Overthinking is diffused by exploring the thoughts to gain more control on them. Essentially, it's reframing those thoughts to be more positive. In addition, we looked at some more ways to deal with negative thoughts. Those included challenging your thoughts, focusing on your feelings, socializing, maintaining great health, having fun and distraction. We also looked at journaling and cognitive restructuring which can help to modify your thoughts so that you become better at managing the conditions and causes of overthinking. All of these as direct results can give you increased optimism to help you to deal with addictions and in turn more confidence. In that chapter you can find the steps to cognitive restructuring to gain the benefits immediately.

Moving forwards, we took it up a notch and explored positivity. Now this is something that's thrown around a lot these days but for a good reason. We also explored the states of optimism and pessimism and how they can again impact on your health and overthinking. Naturally we concluded that positive thinking is a much better way of thinking. That begins with positive and correct self-talk. We have to realize that the mind is always going to keep producing thoughts and we need to take responsibility to make sure that those are the right thoughts. Positive ones are much better. In that chapter we explored curating positive influences so that you're constantly filling and receiving positive influences in your life instead of being a victim of the negativity in the world. Truth is that there's so much to be grateful for. Change the channel and tune into positive inputs.

Additionally in this chapter we explored self-esteem and how it plays a key role in mental wellness and overthinking. We explored how to improve your self-esteem and how to work on improving any negative self-esteem issues. In that chapter you will find specific ways to improve your self-esteem, grow your strengths to become your own best friend. In addition, you can find some useful information about the hierarchy of needs which plays a crucial role in self-esteem.

Moving on we explored more techniques, tactics and mindsets, beginning with meditation and mindfulness. Many of the concepts in this book stem from the concepts of mediation and mindfulness. Both have been proven again and again to improve brain focus and function. They are an excellent remedy to overthinking and in turn a better quality of life in general. We explored how to implement mindfulness along with meditation into your daily life. Then you can enjoy the benefits right away. These are simple but highly effective skills and concepts that few people really master or utilize.

With daily practice they can effectively cure your overthinking. Live in the present moment and it will become easier to break free from what happened in the past or what might happen in the future.

In the next chapter we looked at more techniques, tactics and mindsets to improve your brain function and to deal with overthinking more effectively. First, we looked at self-awareness as a way to be more in the present moment. Great stuff. Again, we looked at challenging your own thinking with questions. Then we looked at thinking big which is an excellent way to make your thoughts much more personal purposeful. Furthermore, we took a look at how distraction, philosophical razors and changing your stories can all lead to a more effective way of thinking. Finally, we looked at how exercise, journaling, setting goals and so on will lead you to a more purposeful way of life. In effect these reduce your overthinking since there's more purpose and more doing what you love.

Additionally at the end of that chapter we explored mental toughness which is a tool used by professional athletes and business people. It is something that sets those successful people apart from the rest and contributes to influencing their success. In fact, this can be used by anyone to produce higher results in work, sports and life. We concluded that it can be learnt by anyone and in that chapter, you can find out just how mental toughness can be applied to you. Overcome the challenges and deal with overthinking to help you focus on what matters. This will help you connect with your life purpose and stop overthinking.

Achieving success can be difficult. You'll be faced with ups and downs. Overthinking can be a major obstacle. But through the knowledge in this book, you can rise above it. Declutter your mind and take responsibility for what you put into it. Stay healthy and practice positive habits. When the going gets tough the tough get going.

Revisit this book or a particular chapter again and again. You may see things from a new perspective. You may gain new insights. Or you may find a solution to a problem you're facing right now. The one thing that I would like you to take away from this book is that you are in control of your destiny. No longer do you need to be a victim of overthinking. What was presented in this book was an effective diagnosis and solutions. It is a new way of life.

Now take hold of the reins of your new life and venture out into the world a better you.

REFERENCES

WAY OF THE STOIC: LIFE LESSONS FROM STOICISM TO STRENGTHEN YOUR CHARACTER, BUILD MENTAL TOUGHNESS, EMOTIONAL RESILIENCE, MINDSET, SELF-DISCIPLINE & WISDOM

Aurelius, M., & Hammond, M. (2006). Meditations (Penguin Classics). Penguin Classics.

E., & Dobbin, R. (2008). Discourses and Selected Writings (Penguin Classics) (1st ed.). Penguin Classics.

E., & Long, G. (2004). Enchiridion (Dover Thrift Editions: Philosophy) (unknown ed.). Dover Publications.

Ferriss, T. (2009). The 4-Hour Workweek: Escape 9–5, Live Anywhere, and Join the New Rich (Expanded, Updated ed.). Harmony.

Graham, S. M., Huang, J. Y., Clark, M. S., & Helgeson, V. S. (2008). The Positives of Negative Emotions: Willingness to Express Negative Emotions Promotes Relationships. Personality and Social Psychology Bulletin, 34(3), 394–406. https://doi.org/10.1177/0146167207311281

Harvard Health. (2011, October 11). Writing about emotions may ease stress and trauma. https://www.health.harvard.edu/healthbeat/writing-about-emotions-may-ease-stress-and-trauma

Why 'bottling it up' can be harmful to your health | HCF. (2018). HEALTH AGENDA.

https://www.hcf.com.au/health-agenda/body-mind/mental-health/downsides-to-always-being-positive#:%7E:text=And%20avoiding%20emotions%20can%20also,re%20actually%20making%20them%20stronger.

Hendel, H. J. (2018, February 27). Ignoring Your Emotions Is Bad for Your Health. Here's What to Do About It. Time. https://time.com/5163576/ignoring-your-emotions-bad-for-your-health/

Irvine, W. B. (2008). A Guide to the Good Life: The Ancient Art of Stoic Joy (1st ed.). Oxford University Press.

Irvine, W. B. (2007). On Desire: Why We Want What We Want (New Ed). Oxford University Press.

Laertius, D., & Hicks, R. D. (1925). Diogenes Laertius: Lives of Eminent Philosophers, Volume I, Books 1–5 (Loeb Classical Library No. 184). Harvard University Press.

Seneca, L. A., & Campbell, R. (1969). Letters from a Stoic (Penguin Classics) (Reprint ed.). Penguin Books.

Stoic Week 2018 part 3. (2021, September 10). Modern Stoicism. https://modernstoicism.com/report/stoic-week-2018-part-3/

WAY OF THE SPARTAN: LIFE LESSONS TO STRENGTHEN YOUR CHARACTER, BUILD MENTAL TOUGHNESS, MINDSET, SELF-DISCIPLINE & A HEALTHY BODY

C., & Lau, D. C. (1998). The Analects (Penguin Classics) (1st ed.). Penguin Classics.

Cpa, L. S. L., & Reid, G. (2019). Three Feet from Gold: Turn Your Obstacles into Opportunities! (Think and Grow Rich) (Official Publication of the Napoleon Hill Foundation) (Reprint ed.). Sound Wisdom.

Gracie, R., Maguire, P., & Willink, J. (2021). Breathe: A Life in Flow. Dey Street Books.

H., Cartledge, P., & Holland, T. (2015). The Histories: (Penguin Classics Deluxe Edition) (Reprint ed.). Penguin Classics.

Hackett, W. (2016). Socrates: The Best of Socrates: The Founding Philosophies of Ethics, Virtues & Life (3rd ed.). CreateSpace Independent Publishing Platform.

Jordan, M. (2019, January 7). The Mindset of a Champion: Visualization. CrossFit 1088. https://crossfit1088.com/visualization/

Merriam-Webster. (2020). Merriam-Webster's Dictionary and Thesaurus, New Edition, (Trade Paperback) 2020 Copyright (Newest ed.). Merriam-Webster, Inc.

P., Talbert, R. J. A., & Pelling, C. (2005). On Sparta (Penguin Classics) (Revised ed.). Penguin Classics.

Press, Covenant, & Coalition, C. C. (2020). The Holy Bible: Literal Standard Version (LSV), 2020. Covenant Press.

Shaw, R. (2016). Cus D'Amato: Life Lessons On Will, Skill, Discipline & Psychological Warfare From Mike Tyson's Mentor. CreateSpace Independent Publishing Platform.

Snyder, Z. (Director). Miller, F (Writer) (2007). 300 [Film]. Warner Bros. Pictures.

Willink, J. (2020). Discipline Equals Freedom: Field Manual Mk1-MOD1. St. Martin's Press.

Willink, J. (2017). Extreme Ownership: How U.S. Navy SEALs Lead and Win (1st ed.). St. Martin's Press.

OVERTHINKING: HOW TO STOP OVERTHINKING, ESCAPE NEGATIVE THOUGHTS, DECLUTTER YOUR MIND, RELIEVE STRESS & ANXIETY, BUILD MENTAL TOUGHNESS & LIVE FULLY

12 Rules for Life: An Antidote to Chaos. (2018). Allen Lane.

Ackerman, C. E. (2020, December 14). How Does Acceptance And Commitment

Therapy (ACT) Work? PositivePsychology.Com. https://positivepsychology.com/act-acceptance-and-commitment-therapy/

Ali, M. (1978). Ali: Born Again! Newsweek, 4–10.

American Psychological Association, A. P. A. (n.d.). Anxiety. https://Www.Apa.Org/ https://www.apa.org/topics/anxiety

Cameron, K., & Caza, A. (2008). Positive Organizational Scholarship: What Does it Achieve? SSRN Electronic Journal. Published. https://doi.org/10.2139/ssrn.1295299

Dar, K. A., & Iqbal, N. (2014). Worry and Rumination in Generalized Anxiety Disorder and Obsessive Compulsive Disorder. The Journal of Psychology, 149(8), 866–880. https://doi.org/10.1080/00223980.2014.986430

Depression: Facts, Statistics, and You. (2018). Health Line. https://www.healthline.com/health/depression/facts -statistics-infographic

Ellis, A., Harper, R. A., & Powers, M. (1975). A Guide to Rational Living (3rd ed.). Wilshire Book Company. Cognitive Restructuring

Ferriss, T., & Schwarzenegger, A. (2016). TOOLS OF TITANS. Penguin Random House UK.

Frankl, V. E. (2004). Man's Search for Meaning (New Ed). Ebury Pr.

Harvard Health. (2011, October 11). Writing about emotions may ease stress and trauma. https://www.health.harvard.edu/healthbeat/writing-about-emotions-may-ease-stress-and-trauma

Hölzel, B. K., Carmody, J., Vangel, M., Congleton, C., Yerramsetti, S. M., Gard, T., &

Lazar, S. W. (2011). Mindfulness practice leads to increases in regional brain gray matter density. Psychiatry Research: Neuroimaging, 191(1), 36–43. https://doi.org/10.1016/j.pscychresns.2010.08.006

Jordan, H. (2020). [interview quote circa 2020]. Interview with Jordan Hoechlin.

Kabat-Zinn, J. (2005). Wherever You Go, There You Are: Mindfulness Meditation in Everyday Life (10th ed.). Hachette Books.

Lazar, S. W., Kerr, C. E., Wasserman, R. H., Gray, J. R., Greve, D. N., Treadway, M. T., McGarvey, M., Quinn, B. T., Dusek, J. A., Benson, H., Rauch, S. L., Moore, C. I., &

Fischl, B. (2005). Meditation experience is associated with increased cortical thickness.

NeuroReport, 16(17), 1893–1897. https://doi.org/10.1097/01.wnr.0000186598.66243.19

Lee, B. (1973). [interview quote circa 1973]. Interview with Bruce Lee

Loehr, J. E. (1994). Toughness Training for Life: A Revolutionary Program for

Maximizing Health, Happiness and Productivity. Plume.

Maslow, A. H. (2011). Hierarchy of Needs: A Theory of Human Motivation. www.all-about-psychology.com.

NBC. (2010). Arianna Huffington interview quote. http://inc.com/ & NBC. https://www.nbcnews.com/id/wbna35018305

NIMH » 5 Things You Should Know About Stress. (2021, May 31). NIMH. https://www.nimh.nih.gov/health/publications/stress/

Ockham, W. O., Adams, M. M., & Kretzmann, N. (1983). Predestination, God's Foreknowledge, And Future Contingents (Hackett Classics) (2nd ed.). Hackett Publishing Company, Inc.

Robbins, T. (1992). Awaken the Giant Within : How to Take Immediate Control of Your Mental, Emotional, Physical and Financial Destiny! Simon & Schuster.

Schwartz, B. (2016). The Paradox of Choice: Why More Is Less, Revised Edition (Revised ed.). Ecco.

Schwartz, D. J. (1987). The Magic of Thinking Big (Reprint ed.). Fireside.

Seligman, M. E. P. (2006). Learned Optimism: How to Change Your Mind and Your Life (Reprint ed.). Vintage.

Seneca, L. A., & Campbell, R. (1969). Letters from a Stoic (Penguin Classics) (Reprint ed.). Penguin Books.

Sylvester, S. (Director). (1979). Rocky Balboa [Film]. Sony Pictures Releasing

Szegedy-Maszak, M. (2005). Mysteries of the mind. http://webhome.auburn.edu/~mitrege/ENGL2210/USNWR-mind.html

V., Raymond, E. S., & Steele, G. L. (2011). The Jargon File, Version 2.9.10, 01 Jul 1992. Caiman.

Virgin Records. (1979). Always Look on the Bright Side of Life. Eric Idle (Monty Python)